VENTRILOQUISM
➤➤ for the ➤➤
TOTAL
DUMMY

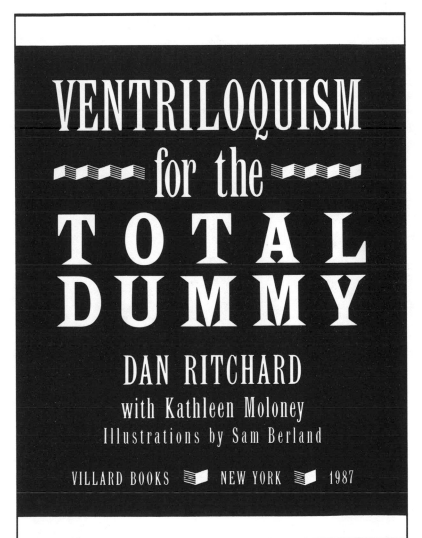

VENTRILOQUISM
~~~~ for the ~~~~
TOTAL
DUMMY

DAN RITCHARD

with Kathleen Moloney

Illustrations by Sam Berland

VILLARD BOOKS ◆ NEW YORK ◆ 1987

LIBRARY OF CONGRESS CATALOGING-IN-PUBLICATION DATA
Ritchard, Dan.
Ventriloquism for the total dummy.
1. Ventriloquism. I. Moloney, Kathleen.
II. Title.
GV1557.R58   1987   793.8   87-40186
ISBN 0-394-75638-X

Manufactured in the United States
Designed by Beth Tondreau
2   3   4   5   6   7   8   9
First Edition

TO ROZ AND PERRY

I am lucky to have a Mom and Dad
who care so much about so many people
and about whom so many people care.

ACKNOWLEDGMENTS

There are so many people who have been part of my life and helped me along the way that it would be impossible to thank them all. But that doesn't mean I won't try.

Besides Mom and Dad, who withstood years of a budding humorist's butting in, there's my brother, Steve, who used to complain about my jokes and avoid me whenever I pulled out a deck of cards. He motivated me to do better. My love and appreciation to Lois, who inspires me to be the best I can be, and forgives me when I'm not. My love to Josh, photographer and technical assistant, and Danny, budding comic and musician, who both cheer me on; to Andrea, for all her support; and Jenelle, Michael, Jonathan, and Lisa, all in show business and always my best audience.

I thank Paul Winchell and Jerry Mahoney, who started it all for me; Cheryl D. August, for her insight into comedy and for seeing the humor in life; and Ellen S. Sandry, childhood friend, champion of endangered species, and poet, for her encouragement.

Thanks also to Antoinette Deutch Kleinman of F.A.M.E. (Future American Magical Entertainers) and to the members who have particularly enhanced my life: Tom McLaughlin, who helped make Conrad (affectionately known as "The Bird") a reality; Bob Yorburg, event coordinator *par excellence,* for his friendship through thick and thin; and Michael Berlant. One other member to whom I'm especially grateful is Julian Olf, whom I knew as an English professor. He told me not to turn my back on writing.

Thanks to Bill Schmeelk of Wellington Enterprises, where illusions become reality, for our many consultations; to all my friends at the Puppetry Guild of Greater New York for their feedback and support through my many years of officership; to Lillian Oppenheimer, Lenny Suib, Billie Nielsen, Marilyn Iarusso, Mary Churchill, and Paul Vincent Davis for giving puppetry a place to charm audiences; and to Alice May Hall, for charming them and inspiring us all.

I'm grateful to Margaret Hinkson, who turned a teenage performer loose on an unsuspecting public for several summers; to Judie Berke for her perceptive suggestions and direction at the beginning of my career; to my industrial arts instructors and colleagues, especially Howie Sasson, Bob Ezrol, Bernie Bernstein, and Herb Schacter; to fellow ventriloquists Todd Stockman, cabaret virtuoso; Stan Burns, historian; and George Schindler, author, for his kind words; to Lee Glickstein, Lynn Grasberg, and Joy-Lily of Laugh Tanks for contributing a routine; and to the one and only Allynn Gooen for his friendship, support, and wisdom.

I appreciate the help of Henry McCormick, Robert Fritz, Helen Drusine, and Bill Myles, who set me on the path.

Even though I've never met either of them, I'd like to thank Bob Newhart and Steve Allen. They've both inspired me—Newhart because he's so funny on the telephone *without* ventriloquism and Allen because his real "funny fone call" premise freed me to be funny with a telephone voice.

There are many people responsible for the book that you now hold in your hands: our editor, Peter Gethers, who came up with the idea (and the title) in the first place; our agents, David Meth and Dominick Abel; and other Villard staff members, including editor Laura Godfrey, editorial assistant Heather Lehr, and design director Naomi Osnos. We appreciate their expertise and their enthusiasm very much. We also appreciate the illustrations of Sam Berland.

Finally, I'd like to thank a few people who aren't able to read these words: Grandma Gussie, who listened to a four-year-old boy weave endless stories and who watched plotless puppet shows with love and patience; the incomparable and sorely missed Al Flosso, the Coney Island Faker, who appreciated my style and gave me advice about show business; Paul Staedlman, who took a moment to change a life; David Beckett, for his insight; Frank Hughes, for teaching me some magic; and Sandra Landi, who was one of the first to have faith in me and showed it by booking my first shows.

For them all, I pass it on.

CONTENTS

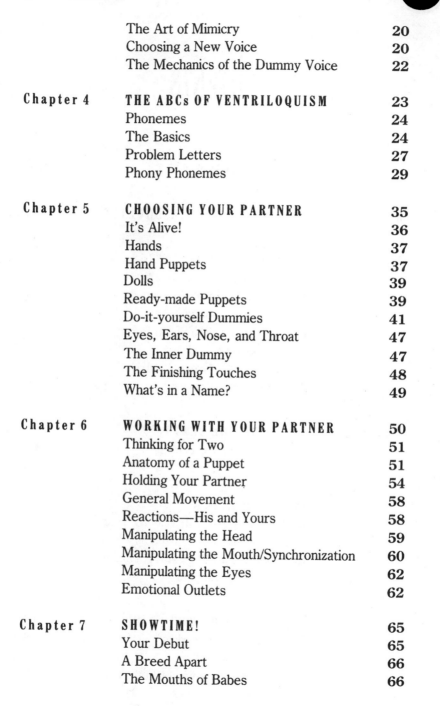

THE WORLD'S BEST VENTRILOQUISM JOKE

Back in the early 1920s, when vaudeville was all but dead, an enterprising ventriloquist decided it was time to change careers. He opened up a storefront and billed himself as The Great Mah Jong, a spiritual medium from the East. His specialty was talking to the dead.

One afternoon a well-heeled society matron entered the store and asked to speak to her dear departed husband Edgar. The Great Mah Jong went into his "trance," and for the next half hour the woman communicated happily with Edgar. After the seance was over, extremely pleased with the results, the woman asked the Great Mah Jong what his fee was. He said it was $10. She handed him a $50 bill and told him to keep the change.

The matron then asked if she might come again to talk to her husband. The Great Mah Jong answered without hesitation: "Lady, for a tip like that you can talk to him while I drink a glass of water!"

INTRODUCTION

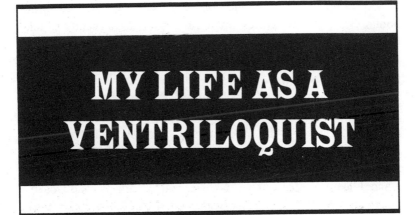

MY LIFE AS A VENTRILOQUIST

Whenever I have to fill out applications or forms and I come to the blank marked "occupation," I'm reminded that I'm not exactly in a run-of-the-mill profession. And I've been asked more than once what a nice boy like me is doing in a job like this.

Like a lot of kids, as a toddler I played with sock puppets that my Dad made for me, and later I watched, mesmerized, as Jerry Mahoney got the best of Paul Winchell on *The Paul Winchell–Jerry Mahoney Show*. I had a vague idea that "Winch," as Jerry called him, was doing the voice, but it seemed to me that Jerry was pretty much his own man.

When I was in second grade, my folks gave me a toy Jerry

Mahoney, and that's when I got serious. Jerry and I were insepa- rable. In fact, I practiced so much—making him talk by pulling the string that came out of the back of his neck—that I actually wore out several strings.

After I mastered the art of moving Jerry's lips, I started working on keeping my own from moving. I eventually got the knack (or at least I *thought* I did), so I moved on to the next step: writing a script, composed pretty much of jokes that I got out of library books. Then, having gotten my act together, I was ready to take it on the road.

My first performance was for a class party at school, and I have to say I knocked 'em dead. (One of the special crowd pleasers was, "How do you like school, Jerry?" "Closed," he answered.) My fellow second-graders cheered so loudly that I took an encore next door, in front of the third-graders. They liked me too.

Most kids have a way of changing passions every few weeks, and I was no exception. Over the next few years I discovered that while I liked ventriloquism, I *loved* magic. Again, Dad got me started by teaching me a few tricks, and TV took over from there, especially Mark Wilson's *Magic Land of Allakazam.* Then my Aunt Dottie came through with a real magic set, and I never looked back.

I wore out the patience of my relatives as I made their keys disappear or coins come out of their ears, but I didn't get "serious" about magic until high school, when I joined F.A.M.E., Future American Magical Entertainers. I used to do magic for patients at local hospitals, but by then I had pretty well abandoned ventrilo- quism—except, of course, for the practical jokes I occasionally played on my friends. My favorite was answering the telephone that didn't really ring and telling someone he had a call. I would collapse with laughter when my classmate realized that there was no one there. Come to think of it, that still makes me smile.

But then I went to the town of Colon, Michigan, and my life changed forever. With its one traffic light and one yellow page, Colon was home of the Abbott Magic Manufacturing Company and site of the annual convention of magicians called, for obvious rea- sons, the Abbotts Get-Together. When I got there, I discovered that in addition to the many magic events there were also ventriloquism workshops and *(cue drum roll)* a ventriloquism contest. On impulse, I decided to enter the contest. Of course, I had no act—I figured that "How do you like school, Jerry?" wouldn't go over very big with that crowd—so I put together a few gags.

You're probably expecting me to say that I won the contest, got discovered by an agent, and appeared on national television a few days later, but I'm afraid it didn't happen quite that way. I didn't win. But I did get something of a prize—a full-blown pep talk from a professional ventriloquist. He said I was a natural and made me promise to start using ventriloquism in my magic act.

I listened to him, and for a while I was a magician/ventriloquist. I did my best to combine the skills—in one of my card tricks, for instance, I'd call up a mind reader on the phone to tell me the card —and soon I began emphasizing ventriloquism. And that's when I decided I needed a puppet.

Early on I decided that I wanted a bird as a partner. I started by deciding on an animal; everybody in those days had little boys as puppets, and I wanted to be different. Once I'd made that first decision, it was a simple matter to settle on a bird. For one thing, some birds actually talk, so it seemed to me that it would be relatively easy for people to believe that my bird was talking to them. For another, birds naturally perch, and that's what I wanted my partner to do—on my arm.

My first bird partner was a good-quality hand puppet (his name was Squawky, and he's since retired to Florida), but before long I wanted to design my own. I'm pretty good with my hands—in fact, one of the careers I've had is as an industrial arts teacher—but I knew I needed someone to help me put into clay what was in my head. I went to an old friend, Tom McLaughlin, with some sketches. He gave me a nice estimate to sculpt and build the bird I had in mind, which was great. He also agreed to let me modify his artistry, which was even greater.

Tom did most of the sculpting, in clay, from the sketches, but then he let me have a free hand. I worked and reworked the bird's beak and jaw (clay is a great medium for the minimally talented), and slowly but surely Conrad Burdee took shape. When I was finally through fussing with the clay, Tom cast the mold, made the finished head, and we came up with some great ideas for Conrad's inner workings. As if the McLaughlin family hadn't done enough already, Tom's mother made Conrad's first costume.

When my audience got a look at Conrad, it was love at first sight. In the beginning he was just a small part of my magic act, but before long he completely took over. My days of being a magician were numbered, and I was on my way to being a full-time ventriloquist who also does a little magic.

Yes, it is a strange job, I'll admit, but I've enjoyed it all. And I'll always remember with special fondness the first time I held a sock puppet and tried to make it talk. You're about to do the same thing. I hope the feeling thrills you as much as it did me.

VENTRILOQUISM
~~~~ for the ~~~~
TOTAL
DUMMY

1

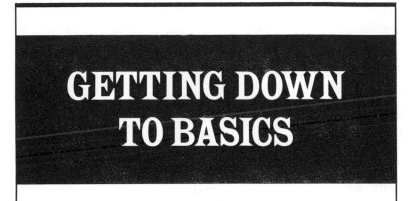

GETTING DOWN TO BASICS

You are about to embark upon an exciting new adventure, and my best advice to you is that you should travel light. Leave behind all excess baggage, especially all the preconceived notions you have of ventriloquism.

I know you're probably impatient to get on with your first ventriloquism lesson—and try out your swell new hand puppet—but before you get started, you need a solid working definition of what it is you're going to be doing.

Over the years many people have tried to define ventriloquism, but most definitions have been inadequate. Certainly the literal definition ("belly talk," from the Latin words *venter*, which means belly, and *loquo,* which means talk) is no help at all. Ventriloquial speech doesn't come from the belly. Like all speech, it comes from the larynx, with a little help from the vibrating vocal cords.

Dan's Definition

Ventriloquism is the art of speaking without moving your lips and jaw, in which additional tongue movements replace all visible lip and jaw movements. Using this system, the ventriloquist creates sounds and voices that, by means of acting and illusion, seem to come from a different source.

Now that wasn't so hard, was it? Now let's move on to some of the basic elements of the art.

The Seven Rules of Ventriloquism

1. Don't move your lips or jaw.
2. Relax your lips and keep them slightly parted.
3. Use your tongue to make sounds. With most of the letters of the alphabet your tongue will operate just the way it does in normal speech, but there are some "problem letters," ones that require modification. We explore those in Chapter 4, "The ABCs of Ventriloquism."
4. Use a contrasting voice. The voice you give your partner—whether it's your lipstick-painted hand or the most elaborate custom-made puppet—should be different from your natural speaking voice.
5. The actions of your partner must be synchronized to that voice.
6. You must maintain the illusion that your partner is acting independently from you.
7. Think beautiful thoughts. No, I don't mean that you should contemplate sunsets. I mean that if you think "bird," the chances are greater that what you say will eventually sound like "bird."

The Illusion of Sound

Have you ever heard an ambulance siren but not been able to tell where the ambulance was coming from? Remember the time someone called your name but you couldn't figure out where the caller was standing? Then you know something about the ventriloquist's best friend—the inability of the human ear to locate sounds precisely.

THE NAME OF THE GAME

In 1843 Luigi Entendanli, an Italian ventriloquist who was also an accomplished chef, embarked upon a crusade to change the name of "ventriloquism"—Latin for "belly talk." He reasoned, quite correctly, that the belly had nothing to do with the art of ventriloquism. In fact, he went on to say, all the work is done by the tongue (*lingua*) at the back of the teeth (*dente*).

Entendanli came up with a new name for the art and shared his thoughts in a proposal that he sent to Italian and American dictionary publishers. Much to his disappointment, however, the publishers were reluctant to follow his suggestions. They told him that even though his ideas made sense, changing the name for ventriloquism was just too complicated an undertaking.

Entendanli may have lost the battle, but he won the war. His worthy cause, though defeated by the Establishment, was taken up by his colleagues, the Italian chefs, who to this day make use of the new name that the Italian chef proposed: *Linguini al Dente*.

Of all our senses our sense of hearing is the least reliable. In everyday life, even when no one is trying to fool us, our ears can play tricks on us. Needless to say, this is a condition of which a ventriloquist takes *serious* advantage.

If You Cn Rd Ths, You Cn Learn Ventriloquism

Anyone who can speak can learn the art of ventriloquism, but some learn it faster and become more accomplished at it than others. People who have a good ear for mimicry or foreign languages or dialects or whatever tend to catch on more quickly, but given time and practice, everyone can do it. And as with any form of entertainment, self-confidence goes a long way. Being a ham doesn't exactly hurt.

Just as it isn't possible to learn to swim by standing on land, you can't learn ventriloquism just by watching. You can learn *about* ventriloquism by reading, but if you want to know how to *do* it, you've got to give it a try. You have to learn some new skills and techniques that will not be second nature to you, at least not at the moment. And you have to do some things that may make you feel silly.

I don't want to sound too much like Knute Rockne here, but I would like to give you a little bit of a pep talk. The harder you work at this new skill and the more time you spend learning the basics, the sooner you'll be ready for the big time, or at least your next office party.

Ventriloquism's Greatest Myth

I hate to be the one to tell you this, but I have no choice: There Is No Such Thing as Throwing Your Voice. Yes, I know you *think* you've heard voices coming from inside boxes, cups, suitcases, telephones, even your mother-in-law, but the fact is, the voices aren't coming from those places at all. They're coming from a ventriloquist. And no matter how skillful a ventriloquist is, he can't fool Mother Nature. The voice he "throws" comes from his larynx, just like everyone else's.

The good news is that even if that voice you heard didn't actually come from the potted plant, it *seemed* to. And remember, to a ventriloquist that's just as good!

A Thumbnail History of Ventriloquism

Thousands of years ago, in a land far far away, ventriloquism was born. Make that *lands* far away, since it's been traced to ancient Egyptian and Hebrew civilizations, not to mention early Greek and Roman times. The only one who doesn't claim to have invented ventriloquism is Alexander Graham Bell. The Witch of Endor and the Oracle at Delphi (600 B.C. —Before Comedy) were probably ventriloquists. Eurycles of Athens did ventriloquial bird imitations.

The first ventriloquists were probably pagan priests, who claimed to have the power to talk to the tree, water, and rock gods. (Today only talk-show hosts can do this.) They had a tendency to wear full beards and to perform their rites of communication at night or in dark caves, with only the flicker of candlelight to illuminate the festivities. They might have been pagans, but they understood show business.

Still, life wasn't easy for working ventriloquists. In the best of times, they were regarded as strange, and by the Middle Ages, practitioners were routinely stoned or burned at the stake.

If there had been a best-seller list in 1584, one of the titles vying for the top spot might well have been an exposé called *The Discouerie of Witchcraft*, by Reginald Scott, the Elizabethan age's answer to Ralph Nader. A well-educated man who had seen one too many "witches" put to death, Scott said that the so-called witches were either crazy people who talked to themselves or ventriloquists. It wasn't until much later that people realized you could be both.

Ventriloquism was first used to entertain in sixteenth-century France (or possibly seventeenth-century Vienna). In 1700, Louis Brabant and his mechanical doll with the movable mouth played the palace, performing for King Francis of the Holy Roman Empire. Napoleon and Josephine were entertained by ventriloquist Le Sieur Thiemet, who used to create all the sounds of a fox hunt.

In 1772 the first book about ventriloquism was published. Written by Abbé de la Chapelle, it dispelled many myths about ventriloquism and described, among others, Baron von Mengen, a ventriloquist who used seven or eight figures, each with a different voice. *Believe it or not!*

By the early 1800s, America had finally caught on. The first American ventriloquist on record is Richard Potter, who also imitated bird sounds. Some thirty or forty years later Horace Goldin created a talking hand (to relive this exciting moment, turn to page 37), and England's Fred Russell invented the first knee figure.

The twentieth century has had countless ventriloquial landmarks. In the early 1900s, Arthur Prince and his sidekick, Sailor Jim (needless to say, the act had a nautical theme), were a top-rated vaudeville act; John Cooper worked with a parrot; and ventriloquism had its first real superstar: Harry Lester. Among his many accomplishments, "The Great Lester" (*né* Maryan Czagkowski) created the telephone bit (see page 80 for how he did it) and, in the 1930s, gave Edgar Bergen his start.

And Edgar Bergen and Charlie McCarthy begat Paul Winchell and Jerry Mahoney, and they begat Jimmy Nelson and Danny O'Day, and they begat Señor Wences, and they begat Shari Lewis and Lambchop, and they begat Willie Tyler and Lester, and they begat Jay Johnson and Squeaky, and they begat Ronn Lucas and Cowboy Billy, and they begat . . .

2

TOOLS OF THE TRADE

I can think of a lot of reasons why I'd rather be a ventriloquist than, say, a harp player or a lion tamer. Two of the best reasons are (a) that I don't have to carry much equipment on the job, and (b) I don't have to feed my partner. One of the best things about being a ventriloquist is that he has practically no overhead.

The most important piece of equipment a ventriloquist needs is, of course, a partner, which I talk about in Chapter 5. Here, though, I'm going to talk about a few of the things you need before you reach the partner stage. There are only a few essentials, and I'm pleased to say that they're all considerably smaller than a harp (and they make less mess than a lion).

Digital Tremor Detectors

These instruments, by means of which even the most minute tremors can be detected, are more commonly referred to as your fingers. In addition to the million and one uses they have in your everyday life, they can be used to detect your lip and jaw movement. Keep them handy at all times.

Mirror

Your lips are notoriously unreliable at giving feedback. Your fingers will give you some idea of what your lips and jaw are doing when you speak, but eventually you'll have to see for yourself. A hand mirror is perhaps the most important tool that a budding ventriloquist can have nearby (which is why we've included one in this book). Your skill is a reflection of how much you use your mirror. One of the great benefits of a mirror is that it's light, portable, and not too complicated to use.

Note to beginners: If you're unable to see yourself when you look in a mirror:

1. The lights may be out.
2. You may have your eyes closed. Try this simple test. Close your eyes. If nothing happens, they're already closed.
3. You may be a vampire. (This is especially likely if you're a night person.)

Tape Recorder

A tape recorder is the basic tool for the audio portion of your act. It's important that the sounds you make and the voices you create sound authentic and appropriate to their situations, and the only way you can even begin to judge whether they are is to listen to them.

In addition to using the tape recorder to record and listen to your efforts, you'll find that it's indispensable when you begin to experiment with new voices and build routines. And don't forget, you need a recorder for your Ventrioloquial Archives, where you'll store historical documentation of all your performances. A vault is optional.

Get the best tape recorder you can afford—make sure it's got a good microphone—and keep it clean. I clean the heads on mine after every twenty-five hours of use. That may sound a little fussy, but I find that it makes a big difference in the quality of the sound I get.

Video Camera/VCR

You can follow the movements of your lips with your fingers, stare at yourself in the mirror, and spend hours perfecting your skills with a tape recorder, but there's nothing quite like seeing yourself perform. Only then can you put it all together—your lips and expressions, your manipulation and synchronization, the different voices, and the nuances of timing. For the "big picture" you need access to a video camera and a VCR.

When it comes to buying video equipment, I don't pretend to be *Consumer Reports*—and anyhow, I couldn't possibly keep up with the latest models. The only advice I can give you is to do a little research, ask your friends, and spend a few hours comparison shopping. Fortunately, you don't need a particularly fancy machine; any one that can be used when you're alone and that gives a good clear picture will do just fine.

If you're reluctant to buy this equipment—and it is a substantial investment—start looking around for either a friend who'll lend you one or a place that rents video cameras by the hour, day, or weekend. You won't need a camera at the very beginning of your ventriloquism career—you don't want to get discouraged—but before too long you'll have an irresistible desire to see how you're going to look on *Entertainment Tonight.*

Relaxation, Part 1: Increasing Your S.Q.

One of the most important items in the ventriloquist's toolbox is something that you can't even see, but you can't get very far without it. It's the ability to relax.

Let's face it. If you're going to spend your time talking to an inanimate object and trying to convince people that it's talking back to you, the last thing in the world you need is to be tense. You simply *have* to be relaxed. The best way to relax is to try to recapture some of your childlike aspects. (Not child*ish*, mind you. Temper tantrums, refusing to eat your spinach, and holding your breath until you turn blue don't help you in ventriloquism.) It's essential to rediscover that part of you that is playful, that enjoys pretending. In short, it's time to increase your Silliness Quotient.

S.Q. Exercise No. 1

Sit comfortably and take a deep breath. Let the air out as slowly as you can. Repeat this a few times. Now smile the biggest smile you can imagine. The Three Stooges may come in handy here. If you have real trouble bringing up the big grin, try thinking of the workout scene in *The Nutty Professor.*

S.Q. Exercise No. 2

Now imagine you're a four-year-old child with an urgent need for a chocolate chip cookie. Your mother says it will spoil your dinner, but you want that cookie. Start to whine, making sure to raise the pitch of your voice. Repeat after me:

"Mooooom, I'm *huuuungry*! I'm *staaarviiing*! *Pleeeease*!"

S.Q. Exercise No. 3

Now you're an excited kid who's just seen something wonderful and can't wait to tell your best friend about it. Say the following in a rush and as loud as you can manage:

"Hey, didja hear it? Didja? We went bike ridin' and sawabig enormous fiya engine wid lights 'n' a loud horn ya could heara mileaway. Didja hear it? Whaddaya mean you didn' hear it? It wasso loud!"

Relaxation, Part 2: Loose Lips

All the best ventriloquists have one thing in common: no matter what they do in their individual acts, their faces (and especially

---

THE BIGGEST MISTAKE A BEGINNER CAN MAKE

Practically every beginning ventriloquist tries to speak ventriloquially with the lips rigid, sometimes even closed. It's no wonder that it doesn't look natural! Tight lips and a closed mouth don't work for normal speech, and they won't work for ventriloquism. Keep your lips relaxed and slightly open, with your teeth touching lightly. No clenching, please.

---

their lips) and throats are relaxed. No matter how tense they may get during a performance—as they concentrate on speaking in their own voices, speaking for their characters, and reacting to their partners—ventriloquists must always give the appearance of being relaxed. If they tighten up, the audience will know it and won't be convinced by the illusion. The problem is that the only way to appear relaxed is to *be* relaxed.

A certain amount of voluntary tension in the throat is necessary, of course—after all, you tense your muscles when you speak, so certainly you must tense them if you want to play tricks with your voice—but too much throat tension will prevent you from adjusting your voice. Only a relaxed throat will allow you to achieve a full range of sounds.

This leads us to the subject of yet another "tool" a ventriloquist should always have at his disposal: the specific ability to relax the throat and lips.

The first step in learning to relax your lips is to learn to isolate them. These three techniques should get you started. The methods will probably seem strange at first, but as soon as you get into the habit of isolating your lips—and that's all it is, a habit—it will become second nature.

- Start to say the letter *M*, and as you gently close your lips, allow them to relax. Now you're humming. Continue to hum. Feel the sound trying to escape through your closed lips and feel the vibrations in your lips. As you continue to hum, wiggle your lips with your index finger. Become aware of your lips. Feel a little silly.
- Now hum again, but this time allow the sound to go through your nose. Lift your tongue up to the roof of your mouth to divert the sound. Try wiggling your lips with your finger again. This time the wiggling should have no effect on the sound. The feeling of silliness is still there, though.
- Next blow out harder but don't use your voice at all. Just blow air so that your lips rapidly flop open and closed. Congratulations. Not only are you relaxed, you have just invented the Bronx Cheer.

After you try these exercises a few times, you should be left with a mild tingling sensation in your lips. Being aware of your lips in this way is the first step in isolating them, which is, in turn, the first step in keeping them relaxed.

Relaxation, Part 3: Positive Thinking

Somebody once said that there are two ways to draw a horse. One is to draw a horse. The other is to draw the same horse and write the word "horse" under it. The same general thinking may be applied to ventriloquial speech. It may not be easy to explain, but there's no question that thoughts have a great influence on how well you are able to produce ventriloquial, or counterfeit, speech.

It's one thing to say the word "maybe" ventriloquially, using all the technical skill that you've learned and practiced. But if you combine that skill with the power of your mind—if you really *think* the word "maybe" as you say it—the results will be even more convincing. The thought will sculpt the shape of your tongue to create the exact counterfeit sound you want.

Thoughts are very powerful. They can make us laugh or cry, smile or frown. They get the adrenaline going, cause muscles to contract, make the heart beat faster and the breathing irregular. In extreme cases they can cause panic and even temporary paralysis. And the amazing thing is that these physiological changes often take place without our knowing that anything is going on. Messages are being sent through your body all the time. Some are obvious, such as the one that causes you to step up when you come to a curb, but others aren't, such as those that cause the lips and tongue to form speech.

Take a moment and think of the funniest joke you ever heard. Now think of something that makes you angry. Now go back and think of the joke again.

The shift in emotions that you just forced yourself to experience happens automatically hundreds of times a day—when you talk on the phone, read the paper, watch TV, curl up with a good book, whatever. Your thoughts are constantly shifting, with differing effects.

To be a successful ventriloquist you have to be able to keep these kinds of involuntary reaction to a minimum, to be able to control the degree of "interference" from your thoughts, and actually to plant the seeds of thoughts you want to harvest.

Relaxation Techniques

The techniques that work best for me are deep breathing and meditation. In fact, it's almost miraculous what a change they can make in how I feel. There have been times when I've had a hectic schedule, when I've been completely exhausted, but after about twenty minutes of deep breathing and meditation I felt terrific again and was able to perform well.

Here's what I do (but not while driving): sit comfortably and let your body get heavy and sink. Close your eyes and relax each part of your body, starting with your feet and working your way up to your head. Let all tension go. Take a long, deep breath, hold it, and release until every bit of air is gone. (Tighten your chest and stomach muscles and force the air out.) Take a deep breath and repeat the cycle about five times.

When you've done your deep breathing, try this exercise. Still sitting comfortably with your eyes closed, breathe slowly and evenly. On the exhale, soundlessly "say" the word "r-e-l-a-x," dragging it out as much as you can. Clear your mind of everything but that word. If thoughts intrude, don't tense up; just let them slip away. Keep "saying" the word in time with your breathing.

For best results keep this up for fifteen minutes or more, but even a couple of minutes can make a difference.

3

CONTROLLING YOUR VOICE

It's probably been quite a while since you've given any serious thought to how you speak. Perhaps you've had to give a speech, in which case you had to memorize *what* you were going to say, but I'll bet you haven't had to consider the mechanics of your speech—*how* you make those sounds to get your message across.

I don't expect you to become Professor Henry Higgins overnight, but there are a few basic facts about the voice that you need to be aware of before you can master ventriloquism.

How Your Voice Works

Everybody's voice, from Luciano Pavarotti's to Phyllis Diller's, comes from the larynx—also called the voice box—which is located between the back of the tongue and the windpipe. The muscles around the larynx pull the vocal cords, and when air passes through the vocal cords and makes them vibrate, the result is sound. Your nose, throat, mouth, lips, and teeth also play a part in determining how your voice sounds, but for all practical purposes the quality of your voice is dictated by your vocal cords. Fortunately, the vocal cords are relatively easy to adjust.

Like fingerprints and snowflakes, each voice is unique, but everyone's voice has three basic qualities: strength (how much air passes between the vocal cords), pitch (how rapidly the vocal cords vibrate), and timbre (how thick the cords are). The tighter the vocal cords are stretched, the higher and more shrill the sound is that's produced. Ever notice that your voice gets higher when you're excited or nervous? That's because the muscles are strained.

You're probably wondering why you have to be bothered with an anatomy and physiology lesson when all you really want do to is take your act on the Carson show. The answer is simple: when you create a new voice, which is essential to ventriloquism, it will help to have a nodding acquaintance with your vocal cords.

Give Me Air!

While we're on the subject of natural functions that you haven't given much thought to lately, consider the lively art of breathing. Of course, the inhaling and exhaling you've been doing up to now does nicely for normal speech, but in ventriloquism, the more air you can take in, the better. Remember, you're breathing for two.

For best results, practice breathing as deeply as you can manage, using the greatest possible part of your lungs. As you work on your deep breathing, expand and contract your stomach muscles and keep your shoulders still.

The Care and Feeding of Your Voice

Years ago I had a job performing with a summer festival in Sterling Forest, New York, about thirty-five miles outside New York City. The festival provided a bus for its performers, and I'd been commuting every Saturday morning for several weeks. One morning I was running late—literally—and as I approached my bus stop, I saw to my horror that the bus, still half a block away, was about to pull away from the curb. I gave chase, running as fast as I could—my partner and my costume flying behind me—but it was clear I wasn't going to make it.

Fortunately, the bus stopped at a red light a block away. At the top of my voice, across heavy traffic, I screamed, "Hold the bus! Hold the bus!" The good news is that because I have a naturally strong voice that carries over great distances, the bus stopped for me. The bad news is that I wrecked my voice for the weekend. So much for the show going on.

It's been a long time since I strained my voice like that. In fact, even though I use my voice all the time, I rarely suffer from voice strain. The voice is remarkably resilient, but like all parts of the body, it is subject to overuse and illness. There is nothing about the process of ventriloquism that stresses the voice, so if you find you're getting hoarse, you're probably doing something wrong. Give it a rest for a while. If the problem is chronic, have a doctor take a look at your throat.

If you take care of your overall health, you'll probably be okay. Don't smoke, get plenty of sleep, eat a balanced diet, and get some exercise, especially aerobic exercise, which improves your body's ability to take in oxygen.

Before a performance be sure that your mouth is moist. Drink plenty of water—preferably uncarbonated (carbonated beverages give a repeat performance). I've avoided milk products and peanuts (a strange combo, to be sure) ever since I discovered that I have mild allergies to them that affect my throat, but in general there are no foods you *must* stay away from. If I feel a cold coming on, a few times a day I'll let a zinc lozenge dissolve in my mouth.

The Art of Mimicry

Children have a natural ability to mimic voices, not to mention a natural inclination to make fun of people. In fact, it's their ability to mimic that enables children all over the world to learn to speak. But once kids grow up, something strange happens: their inclination to mimic sounds gradually disappears, probably because as they mature, people become self-conscious. They don't like to make funny faces or funny voices because they don't want to feel foolish.

As you proceed with the next step on the road to mastering ventriloquism, I'm going to ask you to shed some more of your inhibitions, and it's entirely possible that there will be times when you'll start to feel a little foolish. It may help to remember how you used to crack the class up with your Donald Duck imitation or your repertoire of strange sounds. If that doesn't work, just try to relax and enjoy the silliness of it all.

Choosing a New Voice

In Chapter 1, in "The Seven Rules of Ventriloquism," you learned that your ventriloquial voice must be different from your own natural speaking voice, but the rules don't specify what your new voice should be. That decision is completely up to you.

What comes first, the voice or the character? Good question. Ideally you'd decide on both simultaneously, but since that's not possible, you have to choose the voice first, since you need a voice to work with as you learn the basics. Don't worry, though. If the voice doesn't fit the character you eventually settle on, you can make some changes. The new voice may take a little getting used to, but it won't be like starting from scratch.

VOICES

Here are some options you have when you're choosing your new voice:

ACCENTS	PITCH	RATE
British	High	Fast
Italian	Low	Slow
Russian	Curve	Cut
French	Slider	Night
Thousand Island	Beanball	Weekend

The voice you choose may be higher or lower than your own voice; they're equally effective, but the higher-pitched voice is usually easier on the vocal cords and tends to carry better. (Conrad's voice is higher than mine, and it carries even farther than my own.) You may decide that a new voice isn't enough—maybe your partner should have a twang or a lisp or a foreign accent to distinguish him/her/it. (Warning: If you do give your character an accent, be sure it's a good one. Bad accents don't improve with ventriloquism!)

Choosing a working voice is important, so don't make your decision in a hurry. You would do well to "try on" a few voices to hear how they sound (time to break out your trusty tape recorder) and see how they feel. Make certain that there is enough contrast between your normal and your ventriloquial voices. Don't be shy about asking your friends' opinions as well.

If you're truly ambitious (or maybe a glutton for punishment), you may decide to have more than one voice—a deep voice for one character and an accent for another, for instance. More power to you.

The Mechanics of the Dummy Voice

If there is a "typical" ventriloquial voice, it's the Charlie McCarthy/ Jerry Mahoney voice, the one that you create by contracting your vocal cords and "squeezing out" the sounds rather than letting them flow as they usually do. You may decide that it's right for you as well, but you should be aware that even though it's typical— and perfectly good—it's by no means the only voice you can choose.

In choosing Conrad's voice, I simply went up and down the scale until I found a pitch that felt comfortable to me and sounded right for him. My vocal cords don't play tricks, and there's no squeezing necessary. Take your time with this and use your tape recorder.

4

THE ABCs OF VENTRILOQUISM

R ight about now I can hear you saying, "I'm tired of all these fancy definitions and anatomy lessons. I want to try some real *ventriloquism.*" Okay, okay. It's time to learn the single most important element of ventriloquism: counterfeit speech.

The basics of ventriloquism are the same whether they're practiced by a rank beginner or a seasoned pro. The major difference is that the pro does things automatically, without having to think of them. The pro is free to refine his performance, introducing subtleties and eccentricities that will make his performance unique. With luck—and practice—you'll eventually reach that point, too.

But before you run a marathon you have to learn to crawl. So start crawling.

Phonemes

I'm afraid there are a few more definitions I want you to learn: phonetics, the science of speech sounds, and phonemics, the science of phonemes—the difference between speech sounds.

Some differences can be very subtle indeed. Notice the tiny variation in sound between "pit" and "bit," "bit" and "bid," and even "bid" and "did." Scientifically speaking, those words differ by a phoneme, one sound. But what a difference a phoneme makes: one sound can completely change the meaning of a word. (That's why spelling words over the telephone can be frustrating.)

Phonemes are the basis of ventriloquism. You have to learn to vocalize the phonemes without moving your lips and jaw by learning counterfeit speech and passing it off to the audience as real. The more closely the counterfeit resembles the original, the better the effect will be.

The Basics

Sit comfortably in a chair and bring three fingers of either hand to your face (palm toward you). Place your index finger along your upper lip, put your middle finger below the edge of your lower lip, and rest your ring finger lightly along your chin. Your hand should be relaxed and still. If necessary, rest your thumb against your cheekbone and prop your elbow on a table or the arm of your chair to steady your hand.

Pronounce the following letters and make a note of how much your lips move by feeling the pressure of your lips against your fingers. Rank each letter from 1 (least movement) to 3 (most movement) and put a check mark in the appropriate column. When you have finished studying your lip movement, go back and rank your jaw movement as well.

To figure out how much your lips move when you speak, try this simple test. Feel the pressure of your lips against your fingers.

Take your time with this exercise. Before you fill in the blanks, pronounce each letter a few times to get a feel for the range of movement. By the way, the letters are out of alphabetical order for a reason—to keep you from reciting the letters by rote and to force you to think about each letter. You've been pronouncing these letters almost all your life, but now I'm asking you to think about them in an entirely new way. I want you to concentrate, not sing.

	LIP MOVEMENT			JAW MOVEMENT		
	1	2	3	1	2	3
S						
Y						
N						
T						
H						

	LIP MOVEMENT			JAW MOVEMENT		
	1	2	3	1	2	3
E						
D						
I						
K						
B						
G						
C						
F						
O						
W						
V						
L						
P						
Z						
U						
J						
A						
X						
M						
Q						
R						

When you have finished working on the letters, say each of the following words and rank each according to lip and jaw movement.

	LIP MOVEMENT			JAW MOVEMENT		
	1	2	3	1	2	3
All						
Creed						
Church						

	LIP MOVEMENT			JAW MOVEMENT		
	1	2	3	1	2	3
Great						
Green						
Just						
Get						
Rich						
Quick						
Ring						
Red						
Screen						
Tree						
Wish						

Now note if your jaw moves down when you say the following words:

	Yes, it moves down	No, it doesn't
At		
Get		
Great		
Raid		
Red		
Wire		

Now, using your mirror as well as your sense of touch, notice whether your tongue sticks out between your teeth on the "th" sound in "this" and "thin."

Problem Letters

If you've been through the lists a few times, you've probably discovered that you can pronounce most of the twenty-six letters in the alphabet without moving your lips, or at least without moving them very much. If you're like most people, you've realized that the vowels are easy. The letters that will give you problems are certain consonants: *B, F, M, P, V, W,* and *TH.*

VENTRILOQUIAL
COP-OUTS

Many of the old books and pamphlets purporting to give you the secrets of ventriloquism weren't particularly helpful when it came to the problem letters. Stating that it was simply impossible to say certain letters without moving the lips, these "experts" suggested some fairly colorful solutions. They said that one way was to cover your face every time a difficult letter came up or turn your head away from the audience—not exactly natural.

On the other hand, I'm not above making things a little easier whenever possible. There's nothing wrong with avoiding the difficult letters if you can. Why say "boy" if "kid" will do just as well? This kind of strategy works well when you have a regular routine, but when you're ad libbing, you have to be prepared for anything. Speaking of being prepared for anything, try the following sentence on for size—after you've mastered the *V:* "Is the chocolate in this vat or that vat?"

I hate to admit it, but we ventriloquists don't have superhuman skills—we have problems with those consonants, too. What we *do* have is a secret way of coping with them: we don't say them. We say something else. And that's where my "phony phonemes" come in. It is these phony phonemes that we sculpt to create counterfeit speech.

Phony Phonemes

Now you can stop feeling like a first-year linguistics student and start feeling like Señor Wences. What follows is a list of substitutes for the problem letters, what I call phony phonemes.

First learn the general rule and then apply what you've learned by reciting the sample words and sentences that follow. Eventually you'll work up to combining several phony phonemes in one sentence. I've organized the problem letters in the approximate order of increasing difficulty, and it's best to learn and work on them as they appear. But if you find you're having a bit of difficulty with one letter, move on to the next and come back to the problem letter later. Being challenged is a Good Thing; being frustrated isn't. Besides, what's hard for one person is not necessarily hard for another. Take it slowly, one step at a time.

Mastering the *W*

The first letter to be counterfeited is the *W*. For our purposes the most important fact about the *W* is that its actual sound is not anything like its name. The counterfeit sound for *W* is *OO* plus the sound that follows, placed far back in the mouth with the back of the tongue descending. For instance, the word *we* is *OO-EE*.

Say the following sentences in your normal speech, using first your fingers and then your mirror to see what happens to your lips.

> When we use words with one *W* sound, we will watch. We will witness wild weirdness, working our jowls outside. Why would anyone allow sounds which always taunt and haunt?

Now say the word "tweet" and notice what your lips do. Relax, isolate your lips, and, speaking ventriloquially, slowly say the words "to eat." Notice that because you are not extending your lips forward, creating a pocket for the "wuh" sound, you have to create an artificial pocket by deepening the extension backward into your throat. A deeper "swallow" sensation creates a counter-feit of the word "tweet." Now run the words together.

The results will be even more impressive if you *think* "tweet" as you say "to eat."

The *W* sound shows up in a lot of unexpected places, and there are often subtle differences between one *W* sound and another that is closely related. Try the following groups:

Sue Ellen	Stu Art	Sue eat	Sue itch	no under
Sue Ell	Stuart	sweet	switch	no wonder
swell	Stewart			

oo ill	oh ay	I coo it
will	away	I quit

Get the idea? Words like "who" are not a problem, since you want an "h" sound, and for aspirated words, such as "which," "when," and "where," simply say "hoo-itch," "hoo-en," and "hoo-air."

Before we leave the *W*, try saying the following with your new skill. Repeat the sentences until you can say them with relative ease. (Of course, you may want to leave your relatives out of this!)

We will wisely use our wily and worldly wise old owl ways. We will outwit our woes. We will work our way around with witty word wizardry within, with one outstanding way which will work wonders. Watching which words we use, we will witness our outward jaw. We will quit clowning around. Onward!

Mastering the *TH*

When you make the "th" sound (hard or soft) normally, your tongue sticks out a little, or at least shows, between your teeth. In counterfeit speech your tongue must not show, so it must be kept at the back of your teeth near the gumline. Basically your teeth are hiding the actions of your tongue.

Relaxing your lips and using your teeth as a cover for your tongue, say these lines;

This is not just a thin theory. There is, in this, a thoroughly thought-out thread. The tongue is not thrust through the teeth, because nothing should show through the teeth.

Mastering the *F*

The *F* is produced without the voice. When you make the *F* sound normally, air hisses by as your lower lip almost touches your upper teeth. To counterfeit the *F* sound replace it with a soft "th" sound, as in the word "think."

Say the word "three." As you move from the "th" sound to the "r" sound, notice what your tongue does—it gets flatter and broader. A *TH*, flattened and with more air behind it, is the phony phoneme for *F*. Remember to *think* "free" as you say "three." It makes a difference, as you'll discover if you recite the following combinations:

thor	thread	thrill	thin	thought	think	thirst
for	Fred	frill	fin	fought	fink	first

Mastering the *V*

The *V* is much like the *F*, only it's produced *with* the voice. Vibrating air goes by as the lower lip almost touches the upper teeth. To create a phony phoneme for the *V*, keep your tongue at the back of your teeth and substitute the hard "th" sound, as in "there."

Say the word "than" and feel your tongue. Now try for a broader, flatter tongue formation, which should sound more like "van." Now *think* "van" when you say "than."

Say the following *V* words:

vaguely = they glee	souvenir = soothe an ear
veneer = then ear	save a seat = say the seat
very = there ee	slavery = slay the ree
vista = this ta	adventure = ad then cher

Now try a few sentences:

> Eventually you will find all the tough letters very easy. This is not just a vague theory. It's a dead giveaway when the tongue is thrust through the teeth. Never let it show.

Mastering the *M*

In normal speech the *M* is produced with the voice as air vibrates the lips, which are touching. There are three ways to counterfeit the *M*.

One is the voiced *NG* combination, as in "hang." The tip of your tongue is at the bottom of your mouth (where it doesn't show), and the back of your tongue forms the sound. Try saying:

> ung a rang
> ng a rang

After a few tries the two combinations above should sound like "meringue."

Another method of counterfeiting the *M* uses the "n" sound but with a flatter tongue. To say "mother," flatten the *N* and say "nother," always trying to sculpt and think "mother."

The third way is to combine the first two. Slowly say the word "hangar" and notice the position of your tongue. This is where it should be as you say the word "hammer," and so far it's similar to the way you said "meringue" above. This time after the *NG* in "hangar," try adding the flat *N*, keeping the tip of your tongue broad and flat. You end up with "haNGNer," a counterfeit of the word "hammer," especially when you *think* "hammer."

Here are a few samples to experiment with:

> haNG 'n' eggs
> claNGN chowder

Now try the following sentences, which use the phony phonemes you've learned so far.

Now we have many magnificent methods of making millions of counterfeit words. Phony phonemes are the keys to realistic ventriloquism. Eventually they will feel just right, and I will use them without any movement showing.

Mastering the *P*

The *P* is similar to the *T* in that they are both unvoiced and both plosive; that is, they're made by suddenly releasing air from between the lips. However, while the *P* causes the lips to move, the *T* is made just a bit farther back behind the teeth, without the lip movement. It would be easy to say that the best substitute for the *P* is the *T*, but the *T* is a little too sharp. What you want to try for is a cross between the *T* and the soft *TH*, as in "thin."

Say the word "thin." Your tongue will probably come under your top teeth, and air will pass through your lips, making a hissing sound. Now say the word "don't." Notice that for the *D* your tongue is just behind the teeth. Now place your tongue as if you were saying *D* and let air pass as you make a soft "th" sound. Now close that gap so that the air cannot pass; do not voice it. You will have a sound that is similar to a *P*.

Try this out with the following words:

pad	pen	pond	poor	previous
prissy	pig	perch	park	play
trap	open	shop	happy	clap

Mastering the *B*

As the *P* is to the *T*, so the *B* is to the *D*. Both are voiced, and both are plosive, but while *B* makes the lips move, *D* doesn't. Again, though, it's not just a question of substituting *D* for *B*. Try to create a cross between a *D* and the soft *TH*, only this time it is voiced.

Try out your phony phonemes on these words:

brake	ball	born	bishop	broke
big	bench	bottle	blame	born
boom	bank	birth	beer	Burdee

All Together Now

Using your working character voice, read the following sentences aloud. As I'm sure you'll notice, they contain *all* the phony phonemes you've learned so far.

> I have now completed even more magnificent methods of making all the phony phonemes, the building blocks of realistic counterfeit speech, which is the basis of ventriloquism. Eventually they will all sound perfect and feel just right. As my lip isolation develops, I will use them without any visible jaw movement. My voices will be better, and my acting will improve. As my partner looks and acts more and more alive, we will share many laughs with everyone. Every great ventriloquist was once a beginner like me.

Once you know the basics of phony phonemes, use them whenever you can. Reciting sentences by rote can be a little tedious, so I suggest that you be on the lookout for more interesting material. The comics pages of your daily newspaper are particularly good for these purposes. As you read the dialogue between the characters, alternate between your own voice and your new one. Children's books with lots of simple dialogue are good too.

5

CHOOSING YOUR PARTNER

I f you've ever performed in front of an audience—singing, telling jokes, reciting poetry, even just giving a speech—you know how lonely it can get up there on the stage. One of the great things about being a ventriloquist is that you're not in this thing alone! You've always got a "partner," somebody to distract your audience, respond to your jokes, and generally keep you company. Deciding who (or what) that partner will be is one of the biggest decisions you have to make. Now you know how Dr. Frankenstein felt.

The figure that shares the stage with you may be anything from a hand puppet to a custom-made dummy. It may be old or young, animal or human, realistic or grotesque, a sophisticate or a simpleton. Remember, a figure is more than just button eyes and floppy ears. It also has a personality, and with that personality (created by you, of course) comes a relationship.

It's essential to choose a character you feel comfortable with, one that suits your own style and complements your personality. Invent a character you won't get tired of. Be careful about stereotypes. They can be unnecessarily offensive to an audience, and they can limit you as a performer. The "dumb blonde" or the "English gentleman" may be good for a few laughs, but they can get tired pretty quickly.

In fact, any really strong personality—one that is incredibly abrasive or terrifically stupid, for instance—can create problems. Trading insults with a figure can be funny, up to a point. Don't get trapped into working with a one-dimensional persona.

It's Alive!

The most important thing about your partner is that it must appear to be living—it must have as much animation and movement as possible. Ideally the character should be able to tilt his head, look up and down, say yes and no, and change expressions somewhat.

To keep in mind the five essential characteristics of any partner, remember the word ALIVE:

A	Action	The character should show some small movement at all times.
L	Lipsynch	The character's mouth must move when (and only when) it's talking.
I	Illusion	The essence of ventriloquism is the illusion that your character is real.
V	Voice	Your ventriloquial voice must contrast with your own and fit the character.
E	Expression	Your character needs as much as possible, both facial and vocal.

Hands

Over the years ventriloquists have made pictures, tables, mugs, and jugs into puppets. In a pinch, there's practically nothing that can't be made to "talk." The simplest prop to start with is your hand—an old but a perfectly workable one. The space between your thumb and index finger becomes the character's mouth, and lips and eyes are drawn directly on your hand (lipstick works very well for this). You might add a little hat, scarf, handkerchief, or doll's outfit to complete the picture.

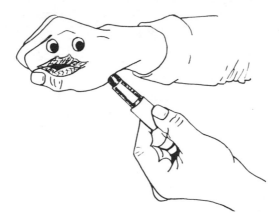

One of ventriloquism's handiest props. If you'd rather not put lipstick on your hand, you can use (and reuse) a glove.

This handy prop is simple enough to create and to manipulate, but frankly, to some people it's not very convincing. It's hard for an audience with limited imagination to suspend disbelief and forget what they're looking at is your hand pretending to talk.

Hand Puppets

This is probably the beginning ventriloquist's best bet, a step up from the lipstick-painted hand but a lot less daunting technically than a full-fledged puppet. A hand puppet—like the one that came attached to this book—is all you need to practice simple coordination, elementary expressions, and synchronization without being distracted too soon by winking eyes and strings to pull.

A step up from the lipstick-painted hand, the sock puppet may be the beginner's best bet. To further the illusion—and camouflage your arm —have the puppet's head coming out of a carrier bag.

If you want to make a simple hand puppet, start with a sock (preferably clean) and get creative. Sew on buttons for eyes, a pom-pom for the nose, a piece of red felt for a tongue, and yarn for hair. To give the mouth definition—which will be all important when you learn to manipulate it—insert an oval cardboard disc folded in half into the sock and use it to define the mouth. After you've fitted it properly, glue it to the inside of the puppet so that it will stay in place.

Leave room above the disc so that you can slip your fingers in above it and leave space below the disc for your thumb, which activates the jaw.

To complete the effect, you can attach some sort of clothing— doll or baby clothes will do very well.

Dolls

If you aren't quite ready for the "big time" of a custom-made puppet but a sock puppet doesn't seem sophisticated enough for you any longer, perhaps you'd like to try something in between: converting a doll or stuffed animal into a puppet.

Simply choose a large doll with a movable mouth and remove the stuffing (clear the room of all children—and squeamish adults —before you do this) and replace it with a thin (one-half to three-quarter inch) layer of foam rubber. Leave space in the center for your arm and room in the mouth for your fingers and thumb. Then you're ready to go.

Ready-made Puppets

It's bound to happen: as you begin to master the rudiments of ventriloquism, you'll find yourself wandering around in toy stores or magic shops, looking for the perfect puppet to complement your newfound skill. When you do go shopping, you'll discover, among other things, that there are several kinds of puppets to choose from, some of which are "generic" and some of which are dupli-cates of "big name" puppets. For the purposes of technique, it makes no difference which kind you choose. The only criterion you need be guided by is your personal taste. Don't be swayed entirely by the figure's looks, though; to get to know a figure you've got to "try it on."

Be aware that when you're buying ventriloquist's puppets, as with just about everything you buy, you generally get what you pay for. The three features your puppet must have are: a space inside the body for your hand; a head that can be turned; and a mechanism that moves his mouth without making a lot of noise. I've seen some "bargain" puppets with strings on the outside that

Here's what most people think of when you say "ventriloquist's dummy." Some are available off the rack, but many—including the ones I work with—are custom made.

actually creak when they're pulled— not too helpful in maintaining the illusion of reality.

Do-it-yourself Dummies

For most people the challenge of ventriloquism is quite enough without adding the challenge of coping with clay, plaster, papier-mâché, movable eyes, and bits of yarn, but a few intrepid crafts-

---

PACKING IT IN

As a ventriloquist, I try hard to have my character accepted by my audience as real. The illusion that my partner is "alive" is essential to my act. Imagine what would happen to that hard-won illusion if I were to fold up my partner and put him in a suitcase on stage.

Some ventriloquists do it—and it's been known to get a quick laugh—but it's just *one* laugh at the expense of the illusion, and in the long run it's not good for the act. At best it's jarring to the audience, and at worst it's downright scary for kids, who don't take kindly to seeing their new friend dismantled and put into a box. Do your unpacking and packing offstage.

Carry your figure in a small hard-sided case with a layer of foam rubber inside. If the case is a little too large, insert more foam or a cardboard partition so the puppet doesn't bang around inside. For extra protection I recommend wrapping the head in a towel or sack inside the case, but design it so that you don't have to slide the puppet in and out of a bag. That can be rough on your partner's hair!

---

persons will want to scale the Everest of ventriloquism—making a partner from scratch. If you take it slowly, building your own can be very rewarding.

If you're one of these enterprising folks, you may find that your creative urge is satisfied by altering one of the ready-made puppets on the market, giving it a different expression or a new hairdo. Or perhaps you'd settle for another compromise: designing a model for the puppet and leaving the detail work to a pro.

The best thing about a custom-made puppet is that you can have it *your* way—perfectly fitted to your hand and as simple or as elaborate as you think you can handle. If you're a lefty, you can tailor-make it to your needs, or you can have ambidextrous controls, just in case you decide to switch hands. And you can also have a puppet that no one else has, with a persona entirely of your own making.

Like the majority of professional ventriloquists, I design my characters and have them custom-made. That way I can feel confident that everything is exactly where I want it, and I know that, technically at least, my act will always go smoothly. And because I know exactly how all the controls work, I can keep everything in good working order.

I'm not going to try to show you how to build a puppet inside and out; for one thing, I don't have room to give you an elementary industrial design course. Here I'll simply give you a few pointers about design and a refresher course in how to have a little fun with papier-mâché. (For complete details I recommend you get a copy of Tony Blanco's instructional booklet, *Building a Dummy Step by Step*. See page 89.)

Models

Even if you're planning to have a professional prop/puppet maker create your puppet, you should at least create a working model of what you have in mind. Drawings are fine, but they don't take the place of a three-dimensional model. Once you've experimented— I've found that coat hanger wire is very versatile for these purposes, but cardboard tubes, paper, even plastic jugs and milk cartons may be pressed into service—you can take your jerry-built sample to a professional.

By making a model I once saved myself from making a costly and irritating mistake. I thought that four inches of space in the head would be plenty of room for my hand, and that's the number I would have put on a drawing. But when I took it one step further and made a wire model of the figure, I discovered that I actually needed five inches.

Making a Papier-Mâché Head

If you want to take your designing adventures one step further, you may want to consider doing a "first draft" of your character's head. If you happen to be an expert wood carver, all you need is a block of wood, a whittling knife, chisels, and a mallet, but remember, carving is a real art. If you're not an expert, you'll discover that it's easier to work with nonhardening clay, which is perfect for the amateur. If you make a mistake in clay, you can add or subtract or rework until you get precisely the look and smoothness you want. Then you can make a plaster mold of the clay head and reproduce as many copies as you like in papier-mâché. (You never know when you'll need a spare.)

There are many versatile materials out of which you can make a perfectly serviceable mold, but the oldest, cheapest, most reliable, and safest one around is still the old kindergarten standby: plaster of Paris. For making copies I recommend papier-mâché because it's easy to work with, it's durable, and it can be sanded and decorated practically any way you can think of. It's also old, cheap, reliable, and safe.

If you want to give it a try, here's a recipe and a few hints about the mechanism.

PAPIER-MÂCHÉ WORKING HEAD

Dust mask
Old newspapers
1 piece of wood that will serve as a stand, approximately 12 inches square and 1 inch thick
1 large box (for head)
1 small box (for ears)
1 broom handle about 18 inches long

5–10 pounds of nonhardening clay
1 small spatula
3 large brown paper bags
20 sheets white rag bond paper
½ pound wallpaper paste
   White casein glue
3 small paint brushes
1 small knife
1 small jar petroleum jelly
   Plaster of Paris
1 small bucket
2 large beads (for eyes)
   Cardboard scraps
   Thin dowels (for eye pivots)
   String or dental floss

1. Spread a lot of newspapers around and prepare to make a little bit of a mess.
2. Nail the pole to the wood to make a stand. (If this is already too complicated for you, you'd better go back to painting your hand with lipstick.)
3. Mount a head-sized piece of clay (about 8 inches in diameter) on the pole and shape your character's head. To save weight and clay, wrap and bunch newspapers onto the stick, cover with aluminum foil, and tape or tie in place. Cover with thin layer of clay. Remember to do the neck. (It should be thin, like a child's.)
4. Using your fingers or a small spatula, mold your character's face exactly as you'd like it to look. Press large beads into the eye sockets. (No, I'm not suggesting that your partner should have beady eyes. The beads simply mark the spaces for the eyes, which will be added later.) Shape the ears and remove them, using a cheese wire or taut string. They'll be attached later.
5. Coat the ears with petroleum jelly and place them in the bottom of the small box. Remove the stick from the head and plug the holes with clay. Coat the clay head with petroleum jelly.

6. Wearing a dust mask, mix a small amount of plaster in a bucket (it hardens quickly). Pour the mixed plaster into the large box to a depth of about ¾ inch. When the plaster has stiffened enough to hold the weight of the head, place the head face up, with neck level, on the plaster. Clean bucket (don't pour old plaster down the drain). Mix a fresh batch of plaster. Pour plaster around the head until it comes halfway up the neck and head. Allow it to harden. Clean bucket again. Mix more plaster. Pour into the small box until the plaster covers the ears.

7. Coat the face and the edge of the plaster with more petroleum jelly. Mix a small amount of plaster and brush it lightly over the clay face to avoid air bubbles and pick up all the details. Mix more plaster and pour it into the box until the head is well covered. Allow it to harden. There will be some heat generated because of the chemical reaction.

8. When the plaster is hard and cool, separate the mold into two halves. With luck you'll be able to pry the two halves apart with a spatula or putty knife and work your way around where the two halves meet. If that doesn't work, you'll have to saw the whole thing in half and then dig out the clay from each plaster half. After you've gotten out *all* the clay, clean off the entire surface of the plaster with a rag.

9. Now you have your mold (in two halves) from which you may make as many papier-mâché copies as you like.

10. Tear (don't cut) brown bags and rag bond paper into very thin strips and, keeping the two colors separate, soak the strips in the paste solution for about 5 minutes.

11. Cover the entire surface of each half of the mold with one color of paper, randomly overlapping the pieces. Brush the surface liberally with paste and a little casein glue.

12. Allow one layer to dry a little before you go on to the next (it may be damp but not wet). This may take an hour or two or even longer, depending on the humidity. Use a different color paper for each layer; alternating colors keeps you from missing a spot. Keep going until you have

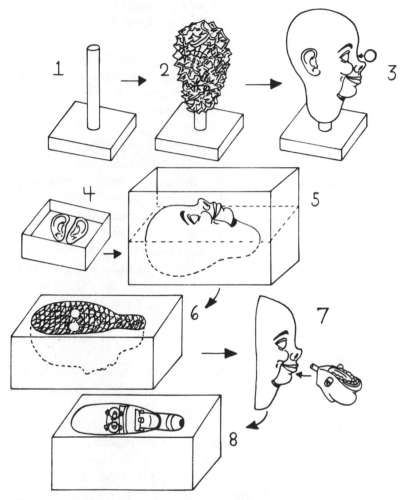

To many people, having one hobby is not enough; they're tempted to take a crack at making their own dummy. The eight basic steps are illustrated here.

six layers. You may work on the two halves at the same time.

13. When the papier-mâché is *thoroughly* dry (you may have to leave it overnight or longer), pry it away carefully, again gently working your way around where the plaster meets the papier-mâché. When the papier-mâché mask is free, cut out the eye holes and the mouth. (Use the illustration on page 46 as a guide.) Cut a little extra space in the neck under the jaw so that the jaw can move down. Glue thin sheets of cardboard to the sides and top of the jaw so that it can pivot on a dowel through the sides; attach the moving eye and mouth parts. Cut the back half—the "trap door"—off and combine the two halves, reaching inside the trap door to do it. Attach the controls. The outside— the one that people will see—is ready for sanding, a base coat of gesso (which will disguise any imperfections on the surface), and painting.

14. It's a puppet! Send out birth announcements if you like.

Eyes, Ears, Nose, and Throat

When you're molding the head, don't put holes in the nose; just leave shallow dents. Make the eye sockets shallow as well. (The eyes are made separately and attached later.) Shape the ears but then remove them so that they can be molded separately and reattached. (They'll get caught in the plaster if you don't.) You'll find it much easier to touch up and repair, not to mention replace, these features if they're separate to begin with.

The Inner Dummy

Of course, there's a lot more to making a puppet than shaping the perfect nose, but as I said earlier, I'm not going to show you how to design and build the interior of a puppet (although in Chapter 6, in "Anatomy of a Puppet," you'll get a working knowledge of what to do with those parts once they're in place). For now, though, we'll stay with the outside of the character.

The Finishing Touches

Sure, it's the ventriloquist's job to bring life to his partner through exquisite lip isolation, perfect manipulation, and flawless synchronization, but it doesn't hurt to have a great-looking dummy, too. Like everyone else, ventriloquists need all the help they can get. As people have makeup, so dummies have paint.

Painting and costuming a custom-made puppet (or repainting and recostuming a store-bought one) is probably the most enjoyable part of this process, especially if you've got lots of imagination and a little skill. Remember, you want your audience to look at your partner, so give them a character they'll enjoy looking at.

Skin

For "human" figures, your best bet is to start with a base coat of raw sienna and then add white or pink or both for whatever tone you think is appropriate. Use washable acrylic paints and be sure to keep leftover paint around for occasional touch-ups.

Hair

If your character will be wearing a hat—or even if he won't—you may decide to paint on the hair. It's not as convincing as three-dimensional hair, but it will do, and it's easy to care for. The more lifelike hair solution is to invest in a wig. Get the smallest child-sized wig you can find or order a puppet's wig from a costume shop or magic shop.

Eyes

Eyes that don't move may be simply painted on, in which case you would not cut any holes. If you want something more elaborate, try doll's eyes (which you can buy from a propmaker) or glass eyes (from a taxidermist).

Arms and Legs, Hands and Feet

Make a "tube" out of cloth and stuff it with more cloth for the arms and legs. Making lifelike hands and feet is hard even for the most accomplished sculptor. Unless you're a budding Michelangelo, fall back on cotton-stuffed gloves and shoes. Doll hands may also be used.

Costumes

When it comes to dressing your character, anything—or almost anything—goes. Naturally, all clothes in the upper body must have an opening in the back so you can put your hand inside to operate the controls. Doll or infant clothing may be altered with very little trouble, or you can find a seamstress who enjoys a challenge and has always wanted to be in show business. If you have patterns made professionally, tuck them away with your extra paints.

What's in a Name?

Once you've decided what your character looks like and what its personality is, it's time to give it a name. In some ways naming your partner is the hardest step of all. The best advice I can give (besides suggesting that you not pick a name that starts with the letter *B, F, M, P, V,* or *W*) is to choose a name that fits your character and isn't too gimmicky. Some people think that a character's name has to be funny, but I don't agree. Besides, what's funny today may be a lot less funny six months from now.

Give it a lot of thought. Look in the phone book, read the comic strips, buy a "name your baby" book, list all the teachers you had in elementary school, and go through your high school yearbook. Then pick the name that's just right for your new partner. Note: if you still can't decide, you can always fall back on the old ventriloquist's standby name—Woody!

6

WORKING WITH YOUR PARTNER

Remember how, when you were a kid, you used to try rubbing your tummy and patting your head at the same time? That's what ventriloquism feels like sometimes. It's a unique combination of skills, and not only do you have to be good at all of them, you have to do them all at once!

Now that you've become an expert at lip isolation and counterfeit speech (if you haven't, return immediately to Chapters 3 and 4. Do not pass Go, and do not collect $200), it's time to master the manipulation of your figure. Don't be too worried, though. That's just a fancy way of saying "learn how to work your puppet."

Thinking for Two

You are responsible for your puppet's actions, and your chief responsibility is to make him seem alive. From now on you must talk for two, react for two, even think for two. Be grateful you don't have to put him through college.

Anatomy of a Puppet

Hand puppets (like the one that came with this book) have only a couple of working parts—run by your thumb and fingers—which

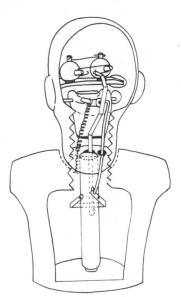

This cross section of a working head gives you a rare look at the "inner puppet." (Caution: Some portions of this drawing may not be suitable for children.)

is why they make great starter puppets. "Official" ventriloquist's knee figures/dummies have several basic features:

The Access Door

This is a removable cut-out in the back of the head that is usually covered by a wig or a hat. It permits access to the mechanisms inside the puppet's head.

The Control Stick or Head Stick

The large bar descending from the neck acts as a handle to control the movements of the head. Here's where the levers that operate the mouth, eyes, and other parts are attached. Old-fashioned puppets had strings and rings here instead of levers, but levers are much less awkward to use.

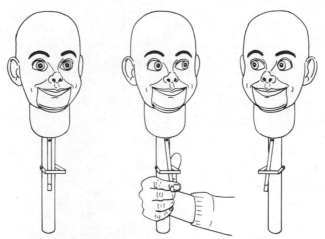

This puppet's eyes are operated by means of a lever. When the ventriloquist pulls the lever, the eyes move to the right or left.

The Eyes

The basic movement of the eyes is to turn left and right, and they are often operated by means of a spring. In repose the puppet is looking left—where the (right-handed) ventriloquist is—so that when the ventriloquist pulls the lever, his partner looks to the right. For obvious reasons this can be tough on southpaws, and many have this part of the mechanism altered. Some puppets' eyes are "self-centering"; they normally look straight ahead and must be moved left or right.

The Mouth
The traditional figure has a moving jaw that slides up and down, with a thin slot that's visible on each side of the jaw and part of the

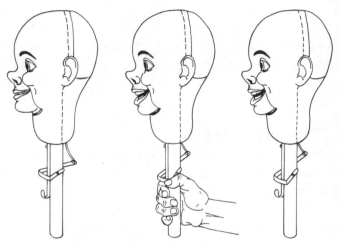

The most important of a puppet's controls are those that open and close the mouth. The ones shown here are designed to be used by either left- or right-handed vents.

neck. (Some have leather strips to hide the seams.) More complicated figures may have upper and lower lips that move, with no jaw movement. Here the lips and "skin" below are made of flexible kid leather and therefore show no lines. In some cases, flexible plastic or latex rubber is used for the whole head.

The Hollow Body
Except for the control stick and the various levers, the puppet's body is hollow, the better to allow your hand to work the controls.

Yours could be made of a simple wood frame (top, bottom, and sides) and cardboard front and back.

The Rounded Neck

The convex rounded neck ends in the matching concave rounded neck socket, so that a rudimentary "ball and socket" joint is created and movement is fluid. During a performance your figure's head usually rests lightly in the neck socket.

The Flat Bottom

The flat-bottomed body allows the figure to sit alone without toppling over. The last thing you need is a partner who falls flat on his face!

The "Deluxe" Models

Some characters have other, more sophisticated features, but the first character you work with should have only the minimum: moving head, moving mouth, and moving eyes. And by the way, don't worry. Those will keep you plenty busy.

In the same way that someone is always hoping to build a better mousetrap, someone is always "improving" ventriloquist's figures. Some of the optional features now available (although not illustrated here) are winking eyelids, eyebrows that register surprise, ears that wiggle, hands that extend and shake, hair that stands on end when the character is scared, and hats that fly off.

Holding Your Partner

If you're working with a hand or sock puppet, the face of your character should be held level with your own and about six inches away. Your grip should be firm but comfortable—don't clutch. The audience will find it easier to maintain the illusion that the character is independent of you if only the upper part of your body is visible.

There's more than one way to hold a puppet. One method—often used by women—is to have your partner sit on a small music stand.

When entertaining friends, consider sitting at a table (the puppet will sit *on* the table) or even setting up a makeshift stage to "frame" your act. Other possibilities for camouflage: have the sock

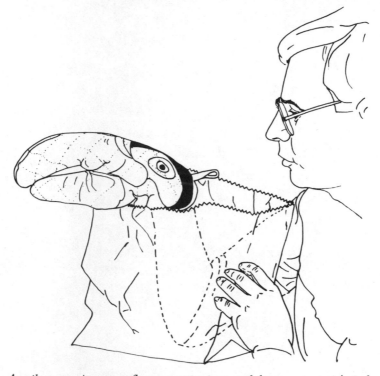

Another way to camouflage your partner and frame your act is to have the sock puppet emerging from a shopping bag.

puppet emerging from a carrier bag, shopping bag, or shoe box; simply cut a hole in the bottom or back and work your hand and arm through until they come out the top. If you're working with a dummy, it should probably sit on your knee or on a table or small stand next to you.

Move around with your character as little as possible. If you find that you must cover some territory, stretch your free hand across your body so that your character "sits" on your arm as you move. (This is how you come on and go off stage as well.) Having your

In the standard ventriloquist-dummy pose, your partner sits on your knee.

character dangling "lifeless" from your hand is bad for the illusion of reality.

General Movement

As you learn to move your character, the first thing to remember is that some part of the figure should be in motion at all times. I don't mean big, dramatic movements but small, subtle ones that reinforce the idea that the character is real. All movements, big or small, should be done slowly, with no quick, jerky moves unless they're in character.

Every movement your partner makes should be as natural as possible and should follow the plot of your routine. When the character is speaking to you, turn his head so that he faces you, (unless he's angry and looks away). When he talks to the audience, that's where he should be looking. When he's not speaking, his head should move back and forth between you and the audience. Again, move slowly—unless your partner is angry or surprised or watching a Ping-Pong game. If a character's movements are too quick, the audience may miss them entirely.

Reactions—His and Yours

Your character doesn't have to speak every minute, but he docs have to be involved in the conversation—nodding in response, shaking his head, looking off to the side as if he's thinking, laughing when you make a joke (for best results give his shoulders a little shake when he laughs). When you're speaking to him, his head should be turned toward you.

Keep in mind that just as your character reacts to you, you must also react to him. (If he says something funny, for instance, remember to laugh along with the audience.) Looking at your partner when he's talking to you and reacting to what he says furthers the all-important illusion: *that's* where the voice is really coming from.

If you're not an inveterate "people watcher," now is the time to start. Study the expressions of your friends and family (you can watch strangers, too, but I can't be responsible for what they say) and watch what happens to their eyes, mouths, bodies, and heads when they talk and experience various emotions. Then try to get your character to do the same thing. The more expressions you can develop by experimenting, the more entertaining (and convincing) your performance will become.

As you work on "relating" to your partner, you'll need to spend some time in front of a mirror or a video camera. To perfect your timing you have to be able to see yourself.

Manipulating the Head

Most of the time you'll hold your character erect, with the interior pole straight up and down and the head straight. The control stick is held so that the neck and head "float" lightly in the neck/shoulder socket. The control stick works partly in reverse: if you pull back on the stick, the head tilts forward (useful for stressing something that the character says); if you push the stick forward, it tilts back. If you alternate, you get an enthusiastic nod.

Other than that, there's not much to know about manipulating the head. Mostly it nods or turns from side to side, as the character looks at you or at the audience, and all these movements are made quite simply, by a natural motion of the wrist. Be sure to make all movements smooth, slow, and silent. If there's any creaking or clicking, try lubricating the character's joints with paraffin or silicone spray. (Keep the silicone away from painted surfaces or they'll be hard to repaint.)

One more thing about the head: some ventriloquists like to use headspins (à la *The Exorcist*) for a laugh, but I'm against them and I'll bet you can guess why. I'll grant that they can be funny, but they're bad for the illusion. And as far as I'm concerned, anything that's bad for the illusion is bad for the act.

Manipulating the Mouth/Synchronization

For obvious reasons, the mouth is your partner's most important feature, since its movements must be synchronized with the words that are supposed to come from there. Synchronization—matching the movements of your character's mouth to the words he's supposed to be saying—is one of the most important of all the ventriloquist's skills.

If you've ever watched a dubbed movie, you know how disorienting it can be to hear one group of words while watching the actors mouth another. If your character's mouth doesn't move in time to his words, the illusion you're trying to create may be ruined. No matter how good your lip isolation and counterfeit speech are, you won't give a convincing performance without synchronization.

TRICKS OF THE TRADE

It's a plain and simple fact that no matter how cute and adorable you are, the audience would rather watch your partner than look at you. Yes, they'll probably want to sneak a peek to see if your lips are moving, but in spite of themselves, they'll be drawn back to watch your partner—as long as there is something there to look at. A smart ventriloquist will take advantage of this fact. When a particularly difficult and unavoidable word is about to come up, he'll create a distraction—a cute expression almost always works—so that all eyes will *have* to be on his partner. Use this diversionary action sparingly.

With hand puppets it's a fairly simple matter of working your thumb and forefinger, but in the more elaborate characters a separate lever, usually manipulated by your thumb, controls the mouth. With all puppets the natural tendency is to go a little mouth crazy at first, opening and closing your character's mouth constantly. (If perpetual motion isn't your natural tendency, you're way ahead.) Do the the following exercises slowly.

Start by opening and closing the character's mouth on each word in the sentences below. Use ventriloquism and your working voice and take it very slowly. There's plenty of time to speed things up once you get the timing right.

"Now I am in synch."

"I like to be in synch."

Now its time to refine the character's movements so that they look even more realistic. After all, humans don't fully open and close their mouths on the first syllable of every word, so why should your character do so? The fact is, in normal speech our jaws open and close very little, since we also use our lips to form words. We do open our mouths when we accent or stress a syllable, though. And that's what the character should do too.

This time open your character's mouth just a little on each word, opening just a bit more on the words that are italicized.

"I *like* to be in synch."

"It's *fun* to be in synch."

Now let's leave the land of monosyllables and try something a little more difficult. Follow the same pattern, opening the mouth on each syllable but a bit more than usual when a syllable is accented or stressed:

"Now I am *fi*nally *synch*ronized."

That's it. If you can master these few sentences, you know all you need to know to master synchronization. All you have to do is keep at it. Repeat the sentences above and the sample sentences earlier in this book (and any others you invent) again and again, alternating with your partner.

As you manipulate your puppet's mouth, keep in mind that the sounds made by the labials (*M, B,* and *P*) and the fricatives (*F* and *V*) are normally produced when the lower teeth and the lips touch lightly, with the mouth almost closed. For obvious reasons it would look strange to see a puppet's mouth open when he says these letters. For the most realistic effect, your character's mouth should be almost closed or just starting to open.

As you become proficient at synchronization, you have to be able to see yourself. A mirror will help here, but there are subtleties that we miss when we look in a mirror. You'll learn much more from a video camera. Even with the wonders of video, however, there are things about ourselves we may not notice, so it will be even more helpful to prevail upon a friend or two to help you with a critique of your performance. Time for a new kind of home movie! Popcorn optional.

Manipulating the Eyes

The eyes on a hand puppet usually aren't movable, of course; they go wherever the head goes. In some professional puppets the eyes work roughly the same way—they're balanced so that when the head turns, the eyes follow. But others have separate levers to control the eyes, and these are usually worked by the index and middle fingers.

It's amazing how many different things a puppet's eyes can do: open and close, move from side to side, wink, even roll. In some the eyebrows move up and down too. I don't have anything against these gimmicks—in fact, I use them all myself—but for a beginner I don't think they're necessary, and I *know* they're complicated.

If you're working with a puppet with a lot of possibilities, use eye motions sparingly, unless your character has a "shifty" personality.

Emotional Outlets

The wider the range of emotions your character expresses, the more persuasive your performance will be. Here are a few of the basics:

Curiosity

Rotate the head as if the figure is searching for something. Or have him look up (move your knee forward while keeping the neck in place or move the neck back a bit) and down (move the knee back) and as he does so, make his body move a little by swinging your knee back and forth. That's why dummies are also called knee figures.

The Slow Burn

Slowly rotate his head and then stop it suddenly as he focuses on the center of attention.

Surprise

Tilt his head away from whatever surprises him. Additional possibilities: his head could jump up, or his mouth could pop open or any combination that fits.

The Double Take

Here the character sees something, turns away slowly, pauses, and registers surprise. Then he turns back to the focus of interest.

The Shrug

Plan ahead for a shrug by slowly lowering the body a little and keeping the head at the same level. The shoulders and the body rise up suddenly, but the head still remains in the same spot. If your partner is on your knee, raise the back of your foot slowly, which will raise the figure's body.

Crying

Your partner buries his head on your shoulder and does a series of shrugs. (Be sure to keep his back—and your arm—out of sight.

Twist your arm only a little and move your shoulder back.) Slightly muffled crying sounds are heard, and you wipe his cheeks with a tissue. There won't be a dry eye in the house.

Squirming
Move your knee back and forth slowly and use the control stick to shift the figure's body left and right. Tilt the head. Add a shrugging motion and perhaps a sigh or two.

Chuckling
A variation on shrugging. The movements are the same but here they're small and rapid, and they're repeated many times. Add the slight opening and closing of the jaw and tilt the head a little. Remember to add sound.

Laughing
This is a whole-body experience for everybody. Hearty laughter is accomplished by the irregular bouncing of the body. The character shrugs, and at the same time he rocks back and forth (you swing your knee). Along with that he tilts his head in random directions and opens and closes his mouth. And just in case all this doesn't keep you busy enough, keep in mind that the sounds of laughter must match the rhythm of the figure's movements.

7

SHOWTIME!

For almost everyone reading this book, ventriloquism will always be a hobby, not a profession. But even hobbyists eventually will feel the urge to perform in front of other people. Like the tree in the forest that needs someone to hear it fall, the ventriloquist needs an audience.

Your Debut

The first time out you'll be nervous, so choose your venue (that's show biz talk for *where* you perform) and audience carefully. Pick a place where you'll feel comfortable—your kitchen or living room will do very nicely, but Carnegie Hall is probably a bit much—and people you trust with your ego. If you feel really insecure, invite people who owe you money.

Keep in mind that no one should expect a perfectly polished performance the first time around. To be on the safe side, though, be sure that the refreshments you serve are especially good!

A Breed Apart

In the old vaudeville days of cavernous theaters and relatively unsophisticated audiences you could definitely fool more of the people more of the time. There's no question that less skillful ventriloquists did tend to go over bigger with the spectators way in the back row than with those in the expensive seats.

Before your first show you'll be tempted to ask your audience to make themselves comfortable somewhere across the street, but try not to be quite that obvious. Anywhere from five to ten feet away should serve your purposes and your illusion perfectly well. After all, you have nothing to hide! I guess that it goes without saying that your audience should sit in front of you. No ventriloquist can make a voice come from behind his audience.

The Mouths of Babes

When working in front of very young children (four to six) is good, it's very, very good. But when it's bad, it's—you guessed it— horrid. On the one hand, kids are great at suspending disbelief; even if their parents explain to them that the guy on the stage is talking without moving his lips, many of them come away absolutely sure that the character was doing all his own talking. On the other hand, if children aren't having a good time, if the act isn't fun, they're not in the least bit shy about letting a performer know it.

Here are a few tips for kids' shows:

- Keep the show short, no longer than fifteen mintues. (Until you're a pro, that is. I do an hour or more.)
- Don't be surprised if all kids, especially young ones, want to do is play with your puppet. (It could be worse: they could want to play with your lips!)
- Keep the humor simple and the topics kid-oriented: school, the playground, ice cream cones, etc. Mistelling fairy tales is a good gimmick, too; all kids spring to attention when you say, "Once upon a time there were *four* bears . . ."
- Kids are very sensitive and easily embarrassed, so be careful if you engage a child during your act. Never make a child the subject of a joke; the joke should always be on you or your partner. Don't make fun of a child's name. You might think you're clever, but (1) the kid has probably heard it before; and (2) it's a cheap shot.
- Kids want to be heard. They don't mean to interfere, but sometimes they can't help themselves. They get very involved. Trying to stop a child from taking over your act can be a big challenge. Your best bet is to use your partner to distract a show-stealer.

You can entertain people of any age with the right material and style.

Stage Fright

Very few people are actually afraid of the stage, but almost all performers are afraid, at least some of the time, of the audience. No performer is happy about stage fright, but for a ventriloquist the problem can be especially troubling. Where there is nervousness, there are usually tight facial muscles and a dry mouth. And tight facial muscles and a dry mouth wreak havoc on ventriloquial speech.

It may help you to remember that all entertainers are basically in a service business, only instead of selling magazine subscriptions, widgets, or aluminum siding, they're selling themselves and, in the case of ventriloquists, their illusion and humor. Here are a few ways to prevent stage fright:

- Know your lines—cold.
- Give of yourself. This sounds corny, but it's true. If you're eager to please an audience, they'll sense it and be as generous with you as you are with them.
- Do your relaxation exercises faithfully, on a regular basis (see Chapter 2), not just when you're feeling panicky.
- Remember that the audience is there to have a good time. They want to like you, and they're on your side.

What to Wear

There's no question that the eyes of some audience members (particularly children's eyes) will be glued to a ventriloquist's throat, looking for some sign that indeed *that* is where the voice is coming from. There's also no question that even the best ventriloquists can't always keep their Adam's apples still.

To hide this telltale throat and neck activity performers have been known to favor turtlenecks, high collars, scarves, and even long beards. There's nothing wrong with these coverups, but I personally don't use them anymore. For one thing, I don't think they're comfortable; for another, I've found that if an act is entertaining enough, an audience will begin to think about something besides the ventriloquist's neck.

Getting Laughs

What's funny? Pies in the face or political satire? "Knock-knock" jokes or Noel Coward? Soupy Sales or Sam Kinison? Woody Allen

or Woody Woodpecker? And how about slapstick, self-depreca-
tion, and saying abusive things to the audience?

The answer, of course, is all (or none) of the above. It all
depends on the audience. What makes one audience fall down
laughing may bore another to tears. And the really wonderful
part is that you can never know for *sure* how any audience will
react.

In choosing your material you can't be guided entirely by what
you think a given audience will laugh at—you have to enjoy the
material yourself or you won't deliver it with the conviction it
needs—but you should keep in mind the Danger Zones of Comedy: ethnic humor, sexist or racist humor, topical humor, off-color
jokes, and very aggressive humor. Now, all of these things can be
funny (if you don't believe me, just ask Richard Pryor, Robin
Williams, and Don Rickles), but they can also be offensive to some
audiences. If you want to play it safe, talk about things that everyone can identify with: taxes, traffic, television, and so forth. And
keep your act squeaky clean.

No matter how much you prepare, there will be times when a
joke you tell doesn't get a laugh. Here's a comforting thought:
stand-up comics who bomb with an audience have to stand up
there all alone, without a friend in the world; but as long as you've
got a partner, you know there's at least *somebody* in the room who
loves you! When push comes to shove, you can use your character
to relieve the tension that comes when a joke fails. Have him look
straight at the audience, shrug, and say, "Hey, I just *say* this stuff.
I don't write it."

Seven Performance Tips

1. ABC: Always Be Coaxed. Naturally you're eager to show
   off your newfound ventriloquial skills, but always wait to be
   asked and then be sure that your audience really *wants* a
   floor show. Watching the life of the party pass away is not a
   pretty sight.
2. Keep it short. Being a ham is good; being a hog isn't. Doing

your stuff for three minutes or so is almost always a safe bet. If the laughs keep coming, feel free to go on for as long as ten. The idea is to leave the audience wanting more. (If you're doing an audition, there is no flexibility about time, though. If they *want* three minutes, *give* them three minutes.)

3. Open with your second-best joke.
4. Close with your best joke.
5. Fill in with good stuff.
6. Pause for applause and laughs between jokes. It's impolite to interrupt, and besides, you need to be heard.
7. Relax and have fun up there. Your pleasure will be contagious.

Sample Routines

Being ready to face an audience is one thing. Knowing what to say when you get there is something else altogether. I'd love to be able to say that now that you've mastered the skills of ventriloquism, you can just go out there and wing it, but I'd be lying through my teeth (no problem for a ventriloquist!). Because you have so many things to remember to do in ventriloquism—lip isolation and voice control, synchronization, and so on—the last thing in the world you need is to wonder what you and your partner are going to say next. There's no way around it: you've got to prepare a routine.

So where do you get your material? You can do what I did when I was a kid starting out—look in joke books. You can read the comics in the newspapers to find character suggestions and plot ideas. You can listen to comedy records. Best of all, you can use your imagination.

Naturally the routines you use will depend a great deal on the personality you've created for your partner and the relationship between the two of you. The main idea is to choose a topic—sports, current events, the weather, the discovery of America, anything you like—and then arrange the dialogue so that you and

HECKLERS

With a few exceptions hecklers are just folks like you and me. The only difference is that *they* think they're incredibly entertaining, as entertaining, in fact, as the performer whose show they're watching. Many hecklers assume that they're actually contributing to the success of a show and are shocked to find that a performer is not too crazy about their interference.

If you're faced with a heckler, ignore him or her. Maybe it (or he or she) will go away, or perhaps the audience will shut him up for you. If that strategy doesn't work, proceed to Plan B: say something to him. If mild, polite sarcasm ("Sorry—am I interrupting your act?") doesn't shame a heckler into silence, it may be time for Plan C: have your *partner* handle it. Suggested comments: "Who's pulling *his* string?" or, "Hey, I thought *I* was the dummy here."

your partner play off each other in a lively, entertaining way. Ideally, you'll get a few laughs along the way.

As I said, you need to work on your own material, but here are a few simple routines to get you started. The first is easy and particularly good for children; the second is somewhat more sophisticated; the third, strictly for adults. They'll all work even better if you give them *your* personal touch. Routines rarely read well; they need acting to bring out the life and the laughs.

In each routine *V* is for Ventriloquist and *C* is for Character.

Sample Routine No. 1

In this routine the character is a young boy or girl, quite shy and not too bright, who takes things literally.

> V: So everyone is off from school for the holiday.
> C: [Shaking head no] Nope, my sister isn't off from school for the holiday.

V: Oh, you're right. I forgot some schools have different holidays. When does she get a holiday?

C: Never. [Shakes head no]

V: What kind of school doesn't give holidays?

C: She doesn't *go* to school.

V: [Laughs] Well, I see what you mean. [Pause] *You* go to school, don't you?

C: [Nods yes] Uh huh.

V: What's your standing in class?

C: [Shaking head] Oh, we don't *stand* in class. We have chairs! And we're *not* allowed to stand on them!

V: Of course not!

C: You knew that! You were just testing me.

V: No, I was just wondering about your *marks.*

C: Oh, they all went away.

V: I meant your marks at school, not your bruises.

C: Why didn't you *say* so?

V: Are you at the top of your class?

C: [Looks up, scans the room, thinking] Nooooo, not quite.

V: Where are you then?

C: [Shrugging, tilting head side to side] I'm closer to the middle . . .

V: Oh, really? [Nodding]

C: [Nodding, sheepish, looking down] . . . the middle of the bottom.

V: [Softly] Oh. [Pause] What happened?

C: I don't know. [Shrugs]

V: Well, it sounds as if something's wrong.

C: Yeah, something's *wrong,* all right. My teacher asks me things she doesn't know, and when I tell her the answer, she says I'm wrong!

V: Like what?

C: Like she asked me, "Where does the sun go at night?"

V: What did you say?

C: [Matter-of-factly] I said it went home to sleep, like everyone else!

Sample Routine No. 2

This next bit of dialogue is adapted from material provided by Laugh Tanks, a San Francisco–based group dedicated to helping aspiring performers express humor. Here the character is a teenager or an adult who's got his act together and is clearly sharper than the ventriloquist.

V: I've been thinking, [name of your character].

C: I *thought* I smelled wood burning.

V: That's what I've been thinking about.

C: Wood burning?

V: No, your putdowns.

C: Oh. I put you down so we can eat.

V: You can't eat without putting me down?

C: Well, I'd have to. You're much too heavy and awkward to hold.

V: I'm not talking about that. And besides, I'm holding *you* up.

C: So this is a stick-up, huh?

V: No, I'm talking about your insults.

C: My insults don't need you to hold them up. They stand up all by themselves.

V: I mean . . .

C: [Interrupting] There! You admit you're mean!

V: I was going to explain what I meant.

C: When you explain things, it's not funny.

V: And insulting me is funny?

C: Well, it makes people laugh, and people laugh at what's funny. And that pays so we can eat.

V: But I have feelings. What about how I feel?

C: Don't you feel like eating too?

V: Of course I do!

C: Good, that's settled.

V: You pick on me because you have a problem with self-esteem.

C: Self steam? What does boiling water have to do with the price of tea in China? Besides, who cares about tea in China anyhow?

V: You're apathetic.
C: Now you're insulting *me*. I'm a pathetic *what?*
V: Don't you know what "apathetic" is?
C: No, and I don't *care!*

Sample Routine No. 3

In this routine the character is a real con man. His main goal in life is to get the better of the ventriloquist.

C: I'm the only doctor who cures hypochondriacs.
V: But a hypochondriac only *thinks* he's sick.
C: Good! I only *think* I'm a doctor.
V: What makes you think you're a doctor?
C: I know how to use an extract.
V: What kind of extract?
C: Extract of wallet.
V: You're quite an operator.
C: You bet. Do you know why we wear a mask and rubber gloves when we operate?
V: For sanitary reasons.
C: No, for insurance reasons.
V: Insurance reasons?
C: Yeah, if we don't leave fingerprints, nobody can identify us!

Two Impromptu Bits

If the desire to perform comes over you but you've left your sock puppet at home, you don't have to miss any golden opportunities. Here are a couple of partners you may find compatible.

For the first—the shadow puppet—you need a piece of paper and a light source, anything that will allow you to cast a shadow on the paper. Just shape an animal with your hand behind the paper and in front of the light (see the illustration on page 75) and *presto!* You've got yourself a partner.

For the second—the napkin and broccoli bit—all you need,

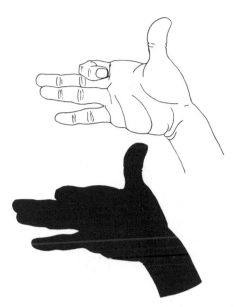

What's a ventriloquist to do when he's left his dummy at home? You can always fall back on a grammar school stand-by, the Shadow Puppet. All you need besides your hand is a piece of paper and a light source.

coincidentally enough, are a napkin and a piece of broccoli. (Actually a third thing, an audience with imagination and a good sense of humor, would also help.) Knot one corner of the napkin and stick your index finger into the knot. That's his head. Spread your middle finger and thumb, which will become the puppet's hands. The excess cloth in the middle is the body. For a finishing touch, stick a broccoli spear in the knot for the character's hair. With this puppet you don't have moving eyes or a moving mouth, but you *do* have moving flowerets! (See the illustration on page 76.)

The Big Time

All over the country, in large cities and small, there are comedy clubs and cabarets that set aside some time—maybe one night a week—for showcases. Some have "open mikes," and anyone may

The Napkin and Broccoli Bit is one of my favorites, although I advise against it if you're having dinner at the White House. NOTE: You may also use cauliflower, in which case it's called the Napkin and Cauliflower Bit.

step up and perform for a few minutes, usually only three to five and never more than ten. Some of the more popular and better known clubs have waiting lists a mile long. You don't get paid in these places, but you do get a chance to know what it feels like to be a pro.

The crowds can be tough in showcases, and there are nights when you may end up strutting your stuff for empty tables and chairs. If you're really good, the busboys will stop mopping the floors long enough to listen. But who knows? Maybe it'll be like me and Jerry Mahoney back in second grade, with the audience screaming for more.

Welcome to show business.

8

NOVELTY BITS

S tandard ventriloquism is great, but sometimes there's just no substitute for the flashy stuff—muffled speech, distant voice, the telephone voice, and the drinking bit. Like the man says, you gotta have a gimmick!

Muffled Speech

So you want to make it sound as if someone is locked in the linen closet or hiding in the jewelry box on the shelf? The technical name for what you're after is muffled speech.

Put your hand over your own mouth and say, "Let me out of here!" several times. The entire sentence will be indistinct, of course, but you should be able to notice that the *T* is no longer plosive, the *M* practically disappears, and the "of" is softened. In the word "here" the *R* is only barely suggested. When you attempt to duplicate muffled speech, that's roughly the effect you're striving for—as if the speaker has a hand over his mouth.

VENTRILOQUIAL SINGING

Singing is not officially a novelty bit, but it is a little off the ventriloquist's beaten track. There's no particular trick to ventriloquial singing, although you may find that in order to keep from pursing your lips, you have to keep your tongue farther back than usual in your mouth. What's more, if you give it a try, you may discover a talent you didn't know you had. Some people who can't carry a tune in their normal voice sound great when they sing ventriloquially. No matter how good your voice is, don't get too fancy in your choice of tunes and keep them short. Seasonal ditties—"Jingle Bells," "Easter Parade," "When Irish Eyes Are Smiling"—are good, and if you're feeling really reckless, try a duet with your partner. "Side by Side" and "Anything You Can Do I Can Do Better" are two of my favorites.

To learn how to carry it off, keep in mind two premises: one, that the farther back in the mouth sounds are made, the more unclear they appear to be; and two, that you cannot sound the plosives—*B, M, P, T,* and *V*—when the tip of your tongue is locked against the back of your top teeth near the gum line. So if you lock the tip of your tongue against the back of your teeth, preventing the small blast of air from getting past, you automatically reduce the clarity of the sounds. (Caution: A slip of the tongue here will result in clear speech.)

To make the "muffling" even more convincing, lower the volume of your voice at the same time.

And that's really all there is to muffled speech—except rehearsing, of course. Once you've mastered the basics, you can get a little fancier. For instance, you can vary the volume of your voice depending on what it's supposed to be muffled *by*—relatively loud beneath a thin blanket, softer behind a heavy closet door.

If it's your partner whose voice is supposed to sound muffled, it's most effective if you start the bit by having the character sound normal and then switch to the muffled sound. For instance, the character could say, "What's in the box, anyway?" He says "What's in" in normal (ventriloquial) speech, but as he says "the box, anyway?" he sticks his head in a box and his speech becomes muffled. It can work well the other way around, too. Start with the character in a box, talking or singing. When you open the box, he emerges, talking or singing normally. The instant switch heightens the illusion.

The Drinking Bit

Myth: You can drink while you're talking.

Fact: Drinking while talking is the same as looking at yourself in the mirror with your eyes closed: it's physically impossible. When you swallow, your epiglottis closes your windpipe to keep food and liquid from making their way to your lungs. When your windpipe is closed, you can't talk. QED: You can't drink and talk at the same time.

In some ways the drinking bit breaks the illusion that is essential to ventriloquism. It reminds your audience that it's you, not your partner, who's doing the talking. Even so, it's one of the most appealing novelty acts in a ventriloquist's repertoire. The trick is, of course, that even if you can't talk and drink at the same time, you can *look* as though you can. Here's how.

First figure out how much water you can comfortably hold in your mouth. Fill a small glass with water and stand near the sink. As you tilt your head back to drink, seal off your throat with your tongue. Sip a small amount of water—don't swallow—and hold the water in the small "well" you've created in your mouth. Keep sipping until you can't hold any more water without dribbling. Close your mouth. Pour what's left in the glass down the sink and spit the water from your mouth back into the glass. Mark the height of the water on the glass. Now you know your capacity—the amount you can comfortably hold in your mouth. From now on, when you do the drinking bit in earnest, you'll fill that glass to that spot. (To make this illusion even more effective, use a thick-bottomed glass. It will appear fuller than it is. You might also use a colored liquid.)

The next step is to learn to hum with water in your mouth. Fill your mouth to capacity as we explained above, close your lips, and then hum—make the "ng" sound and hold it for as long as you can. If you dribble, you're holding too much water. Start again and adjust your capacity. Note that all of the sound is coming out of your nose—a good thing, since it keeps you from choking.

Now on to the bit itself.

You and your partner are talking and then your partner begins singing. Prepare for the last note of his song by getting a little extra air. As your partner hits and holds the last note, *slowly* sip the contents of the glass, humming away all the while. After you drain the glass, turn it upside down to show that it's empty and continue to hold the note. (Your partner may shake a little from the strain of holding the note.) Still humming, with your mouth full and lips closed, take your bow. As the audience applauds, your partner ends the note and takes his bow. While all eyes are on your partner (see "Tricks of the Trade," page 60), swallow the water.

The Telephone Voice

Do you sometimes hear strange, disembodied voices or talk to people you can't see? No? Then I guess you don't use the telephone.

In my act I use the telephone a lot. (I think I've had a warm spot in my heart for the phone ever since my practical joking days in high school, when I used to fool my friends into thinking they had a call.) The phone bit—the illusion that there is a voice coming from the phone you're holding—is tricky because there's no character to distract the audience. All eyes will be glued to your lips, the last place you want them to be, so unless you do it very well indeed, don't try the telephone bit. When the phone voice talks, if the audience sees your mouth even quiver, it's all over.

On the other hand, the bit can be a huge crowd pleaser, so it's worth trying to master it.

The key to the telephone voice lies in the amount of air you release, which is as little as possible. When you speak in the "phone mode," you virtually hold your breath and then squeeze out each sound. You have to produce sounds at the back of the mouth, rather like an extended grunt. Break out your tape recorder and practice. This technique can be tiring, so keep your conversations short at first. As you become more proficient, you may allow yourself to become longer-winded.

Once you think you've got it, try the following sample phone bit. *V* stands for you; *P* is for phone.

V: Excuse me. I must make a quick call. [Reach for phone. Look surprised.] Hello?

P: [Irritated] Excuse me! You're interrupting!

V: [Hesitantly] Excuse *me*! This is *my* phone!

P: [Sharply] Well, this is *my* call!

V: [Assertively] You can't use my phone.

P: [Puzzled] I'm *not*. I'm using mine.

V: [Matter-of-factly] I don't have a *party* line.

P: [Gotcha!] You sure don't sound like much fun!

Distant Voice

Some experts say that there are two voices in ventriloquism: a *near voice,* which is used with a puppet that is held close to the ventriloquist, and a *distant voice,* which you use when you want to give the illusion that someone is calling from a great distance. (As if that weren't complicated enough, some talk about a third, *near-distant* voice, which is used for muffled speech.)

I don't buy it.

To me, ventriloquism is ventriloquism, and distinguishing between voices just muddies the waters, which are already muddy enough. No matter how near or how far away a ventriloquial voice is meant to be (and no one has ever defined, to my satisfaction, anyhow, exactly where "near" ends and "distant" begins), the sounds are counterfeited in the same way.

Of course, there are special techniques for conveying the illusion that a voice is coming from offstage or somewhere out of sight. First, because the character is unseen, the ventriloquist must rely more than usual on his vocal abilities and his acting skill to direct the audience's attention elsewhere. For instance, if you cup a hand around your ear and look in the direction of the voice, the audience will look there, too.

Second, your voice must be modified somewhat. The general rule is to draw out each word, elongating the vowel sounds abnormally. The labials will be less clear than usual, as all sounds will be, but because the voice is meant to be coming from far away, the audience will be inclined to accept it.

Here's a sample Distant Voice routine. You're *V,* and *D* is Distant Voice.

> D: [Yelling to you, but you don't notice] V [insert your name],
>   . . . can . . . you . . . come . . . here?
> V: [You look around]
> D: V . . . can . . . you . . . come . . . here?
> V: [You look around but can't spot the source of the voice.
>   You yell in all directions] Are you calling me?
> D: Yeah!
> V: [You still can't figure out where the voice is coming from]
>   What do you want?
> D: I . . . want . . . you . . . to . . . come . . . here.
> V: I can't right now. I'm doing a show. What do you want?
> D: I . . . need . . . a . . . ladder.

V: What for?

D: To . . . get . . . down . . . from . . . this . . . tree.

V: [Stage whisper to audience] Oh, brother! [Yelling] Why in the world did you climb the tree?

D: I . . . didn't . . . climb . . . the . . . tree.

V: [Exasperated] Then *how* did you get up there?

D: By . . . parachute!

V: I'm coming! [You turn to the audience] Sorry, I've got to go. [Leaving the stage] Hang in there!

EPILOGUE

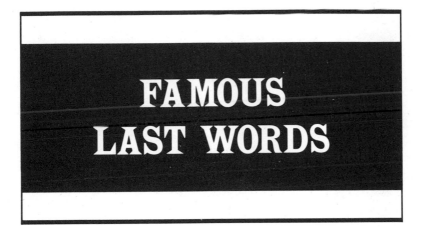

FAMOUS LAST WORDS

Well, we've come to the end of our travels together. I hope you've begun to experience some of the fun and excitement of ventriloquism. Most of you will play around with it as a hobby, sharing some fun with your friends and maybe fooling them a little. Some of you may actually go on to perform professionally. Whatever you choose to do, I wish you the best of luck.

For those of you who do go on to perform, I'd like to share the two maxims I live by in my professional life. They're not terribly profound, perhaps, but to me they're true, and they're important. The first is, Every show is an audition. The second is, The more shows you do, the more shows you do.

And there's one final secret I'd like to let you in on. Many of you may have thought that the title of this book—*Ventriloquism for the Total Dummy*—meant that this was a book meant to teach inept people how to perform ventriloquism. *Au contraire!* This is a book to teach ept people to use all the expression and skills they can muster to *create* the total dummy!

Good luck.

THE WORLD'S SECOND-BEST VENTRILOQUISM JOKE

A guy and his friend walked into a restaurant and went over to the table in the corner. Reaching into his pocket, the guy took out a tiny piano and put it gently on the table. From another pocket he took out a little piano stool. He reached into a third pocket and took out a little perch. Next he reached for a mouse, which he put on the stool. And finally, from his breast pocket, he brought out a little bird and placed him on the perch.

By now a curious crowd was starting to gather. On a signal from the guy, the mouse began to play the piano, and the bird began to sing, absolutely beautifully. The crowd went wild—no one had ever heard anything as remarkable as that bird's voice. Within a half hour, news of the amazing bird had spread, and the place was packed with cheering fans.

Naturally the restaurateur was more than a little interested in the new attraction. Not wasting any time, he offered to buy the extraordinary bird. The guy said he wasn't interested in selling, but the owner wouldn't give up. Finally he offered a thousand dollars for the bird—an offer the guy couldn't refuse.

A thousand dollars richer, the guy packed up his stool, his tiny piano, and his mouse. As he was leaving, his friend turned to him and said, "I can't believe it! You sold the singing bird!"

"Nah, that bird can't sing," the guy answered. "The mouse is a ventriloquist!"

WHERE TO GET SUPPLIES, ETC.

When you begin looking for props you need—puppets or puppet parts, propmakers, costumes, patterns, sample routines, etc.—you should go straight to the Yellow Pages and look under Ventriloquism. Unfortunately, you probably won't find anything there. Next go to Magic Supplies, Puppets, Dolls, and Costumes and start letting your fingers do the walking. If you're lucky, you'll find whatever you need close to home, but just in case you aren't that fortunate, here are a few names and addresses that may come in handy:

Laugh-Makers: A Magazine for Family Entertainers
P.O. Box 160
Syracuse, NY 13215
A trade magazine published six times a year. The articles are interesting, and the ads are extremely helpful for people trying to track down supplies. $3.00 per issue.

Tony Blanco's Props Unlimited
P.O. Box 235
Belmar, NJ 07719
Creators and distributors of standard and custom-made puppets and puppet patterns, theatrical props, instructional booklets, and other supplies. Send a dollar and a self-addressed stamped envelope for a catalog.

Sho-Biz Comedy Services
1735 East 26th Street
Brooklyn, NY 11229
Telephone: (718) 336-0605
They make and sell all sorts of props and other ventriloquist's supplies. Send for catalog.

Maher Studios
P.O. Box 420
Littleton, CO 80160
Telephone: (303) 798-6830
Supplier of all things ventriloquial. Send for a catalog.

Laugh Tanks
116 Coleridge Street
San Francisco, CA 94110
Attention: Lee Glickstein
They conduct workshops and seminars for anyone who wants to develop his comedic style, including ventriloquists.

Comedy Techniques for Writers and Performers
by Melvin Helitzer
Lawhead Press
304 pages
$19.95 hardcover (ISBN 0-916199-00-0)
$14.95 paperback (ISBN 0-916199-01-0)
This is the most comprehensive, practical textbook on the "how-to" of comedy writing I have ever seen. This man knows his stuff. Order your copy from Lawhead Press, 900 East State Street, Athens, OH 45701

The Vent Haven Museum
33 West Maple Street
Fort Mitchell, KY 41011
Nonprofit home of more than five hundred retired ventriloquists' figures, this museum also sponsors an annual ConVENTion, usually in July. Send a self-addressed stamped envelope for details.

ABOUT THE AUTHORS

Dan Ritchard has been an entertainer for twenty years, during which time he has performed everywhere from Harvey Mudd College in Claremont, California, to Alice Tully Hall in Lincoln Center. A magician and a comic as well as a ventriloquist, he gives lectures, acts in commercials, and has made frequent television appearances. He has recently written and produced a documentary about the life and work of Alice May Hall, *Puppets—Fountain of Youth*. He lives in New York, where, at a *Sports Illustrated* awards dinner in 1985, Mary Lou Retton kissed Conrad Burdee on the beak.

Kathleen Moloney has written or co-written books on a variety of subjects, including health, manners, and baseball. She lives in New York City.